S.S. 728.

$$\frac{40}{\frac{\text{W.O.}}{5630}}$$

# NOTES

### FOR

# GUIDANCE OF OFFICERS OF THE
# LABOUR CORPS IN FRANCE.

**FireStep Publishing**
Gemini House
136-140 Old Shoreham Road
Brighton
BN3 7BD

www.firesteppublishing.com

First published by the General Staff, War Office 1918.
First published in this format by FireStep Editions,
an imprint of FireStep Publishing, in association with
the National Army Museum, 2013.

NATIONAL
**ARMY**
MUSEUM

www.nam.ac.uk

ISBN 978-1-908487-67-4

Cover design FireStep Publishing
Typeset by FireStep Publishing
Printed and bound in Great Britain

Please note: *In producing in facsimile from original historical documents, any
imperfections may be reproduced and the quality may be lower than modern
typesetting or cartographic standards.*

S.S. 728.

# NOTES

### FOR

# GUIDANCE OF OFFICERS OF THE
# LABOUR CORPS IN FRANCE.

This pamphlet is issued by the Quartermaster General's Branch in France for the assistance and guidance of Labour Officers; it should not be quoted as an authority in official correspondence.

*September,* 1918.

LONDON :
PUBLISHED BY HIS MAJESTY'S STATIONERY OFFICE.

FIRESTEP
Editions

www.firesteppublishing.com

# CONTENTS

(B 13360)   Wt. w. 249—P.P. 26   5000   9/18   H & S   P. 17/807

# NOTES FOR THE GUIDANCE OF OFFICERS OF THE LABOUR CORPS IN FRANCE.

*(The Organisation and Administration of Unskilled Labour is dealt with in G.R.O. 3502.)*

## CHAPTER I.—ORGANISATION OF LABOUR UNITS.

The unskilled labour in France includes the following categories: —

- (a) The Labour Corps, including—
    - (i) Labour Companies.
    - (ii) Divisional Employment Companies.
    - (iii) Area Employment Companies.
- (b) Canadian Labour Battalions.
- (c) Middlesex (Alien) Labour Companies.
- (d) South African Native Labour Corps.
- (e) Cape Coloured Battalion.
- (f) Egyptian Labour Corps.
- (g) Chinese Labour Corps.
- (h) Fijian Labour Detachment.
- (i) Indian Labour Corps.
- (j) Non-Combatant Corps.
- (k) Prisoner of War Companies.
- (l) French and Belgian Civilian Labour.

The basis of the organisation is the company of 500 all ranks, composed of four platoons, each under a Subaltern. The detail of the War Establishment of a Labour Company varies with the different categories of labour.

In the case of British Labour Companies, when up to Establishment, the strength of the platoons is such that, allowing for N.C.Os. regimentally employed, men on leave, and sick, each platoon can always turn out 100 strong for work.

A platoon consists of two sections, each under a Sergeant.

A section consists of two subsections, each under a Corporal.

Companies are collected for purposes of command, discipline, and interior economy in Labour groups, for which " Labour Group H.Q." are provided ; the number of Companies in a Group varies with the locality.

B

A proportion of all British Labour Companies (one platoon) employed in the Army Areas is armed in order that resistance may be offered if there is any interference by the enemy whilst at work.

It is not intended that Labour should be used for holding the line or for other purposes than Labour.

The organisation is designed to meet the constantly varying requirements of Services and Departments for Labour, Companies being added to, or transferred from, Groups without breaking the usual chain of command.

A Group Commander is responsible :—

(i) For the efficiency of the Labour in his Group, and for the discipline, administration and interior economy for the Units which compose his Group (G.R.O. 2472).

(ii) For seeing that his officers understand the work upon which their men are employed, and that they superintend it properly.

(iii) For keeping in close touch with the Labour Commandant, Army or Corps (or the Assistant Controller of Labour, if in the L. of C. Area), and for bringing to his notice anything connected with the more efficient employment of the units in his Group.

(iv) For the distribution of the Labour under the instructions of the Labour Commandant, Army or Corps, or Base or Area H.Q. (through A.C.L.) if in the L. of C. Area.

No movements of Labour will be made by Employers without reference to the Headquarters of the Area concerned.

## CHAPTER II.—DISTRIBUTION AND USE OF LABOUR.

1. The Labour organisation has two main objects in view :—

(a) To release the fighting soldier for his legitimate work.

(b) To assist the Services and Departments to carry out their tasks.

Nine hours is the normal working day, exclusive of the time occupied for meals and for going to and from the place of work. If the distance from the place of parade to the work is more than 1½ miles, the time taken to march the excess distance may be deducted from the hours of work. For labour of low medical category the normal working day is eight hours.

It is frequently found that the quantity of work executed per man in working parties falls considerably short of the standard which experience has shown to be easily obtainable.

The main cause of this is not unwillingness on the part of the rank and file, but lack of organisation on the part of the officers and N.C.Os. of labour units and the employer.

The greater part of the work on which Labour is employed is not highly skilled, e.g., defences, digging drains, mending roads, building embankments, handling ammunition, stores, timber or stone; this is work that Labour Officers should be able to carry out on the principle of " Contracting " for the employer.

If the Employer explains to the Labour Officer the nature and extent of the work to be done, the latter should estimate the number of men required and fix tasks, distribute the work to his men and undertake responsibility for the proper execution and completion of the work in the time laid down.

The final responsibility rests with the Department employing the Labour, and they cannot be expected, therefore, to delegate any part of their responsibility to Labour unless the Labour Officers show themselves to possess the necessary keenness and capacity

The Employer's Officer should, as a general rule, give his instructions with regard to work for the following day at least as early as the previous afternoon to enable the Company Commanders to instruct Officers i/c Working Parties who will thus be enabled to get their men on to the work with the least possible delay. The Employer's Officer should confine himself to technical direction of the work only; it is no part of his duty to enforce discipline or stimulate the men.

When the system of " contracting out " is not applicable, orders to the men of Labour units should be given through their Officers and N.C.Os.

The Labour N.C.Os. should work with their men as much as practicable, provided that this does not interfere with efficient supervision, and Officers and senior N.C.Os. should encourage their men on all occasions, and increase output by example and instruction.

The Labour Officers and N.C.Os. should therefore become acquainted with the best way of doing their work, whether discharging ships, mending roads, felling trees or handling stores.

Output can be much increased—

(i) By detailing parties as far as possible by military units (companies, platoons or sections) rather than by numbers, each unit being accompanied by its own officers and N.C.Os.

(ii) By keeping the same men employed on the same work day by day, so that they take an interest in its progress and completion.

(iii) By employing task work and permitting a section, or
platoon, to rest for a smoke (except near petrol or
ammunition), or cease work, or to return to billets when
their own particular piece of work is finished. The
spirit of competition thus created has a marked effect.

## 2. *Task Work.*

The C.-in-C. has directed that "task work" shall be employed
as shown by the following :—

Extract from O.B. 1243, 28/2/16, para. 8 : "The C.-in-C.
desires . . . . to point out the necessity for constant supervision of labour and for task work whenever it is possible to arrange
for it. He is of opinion that this is frequently overlooked ; in
consequence much time is wasted."

In some cases it may be impossible to employ "task
work" at all, but in the majority of cases it will be found possible to
make some use of this method. When the task as a whole cannot be
executed by "task work," small portions of it can often be done in
this way. For instance, a gang engaged in shifting even quite a small
stack of stores or ammunition from one part of a shed to another,
or from shed to lorry, say, an eight hours' job in all, will be found
as a rule to work much more quickly if they know that they can
break off either for a spell, or for the day, when the shed is empty.
Where the work is more skilled, employment of "task work"
requires more experience and arrangement, but, with a little
experience with ordinary labour and of the work done by any
particular gang on ordinary labour jobs, it will be found possible
to gauge pretty accurately what they can do per hour, and then task
work can be adopted. Experience has shown that task work is
satisfactory both to the employers and employed.

## 3. *Tools.*

Much labour is sometimes expended in carrying tools several
miles back to billets, instead of forming a dump near the job.

As a general rule, tools will be found by the Service or Department employing the labour, but a certain number of tools are
included in the Mobilisation Store Table of each unit. These, however, should be kept, as far as possible, for use in preparing billets,
&c.

Tools furnished by an Employer to a Unit are not to be taken
by the Unit when it moves, unless it is going to work for the same
employer and is instructed by the Employer that they should be
taken.

## 4. *Getting Good Results.*

Much trouble can be avoided and efficiency increased if
officers keep in close touch with the employers under whose instructions they are working.

Experience has shown that waste of Labour is apt to occur owing to a tendency on the part of the employers :—

(i) To indent for more Labour than is required.

(ii) To refrain from giving early notice of the date on which Labour will be free for transfer elsewhere.

It is essential that this should be checked, in order that the best results may be obtained from Labour.

Continual smoking during working hours is to be discouraged ; it is unnecessary and unusual in civilian work, except where men are exposed to stenches or exceptional conditions. Opportunity should be taken to give time for a smoke when the men knock off for lunch.

All ranks should have briefly explained to them the object of the work, for what, and by whom, it will be used, what purpose it will serve, and, especially, that all the work is being done for the prosecution of the war and is not merely a "fatigue." A few minutes spent in rousing the men's interest in their work is usually time well spent.

A healthy spirit of emulation should be created by pointing out the quantity of work of any kind which should be done per day, and the amount done by other and better Companies.

Above all the men must be made to understand that whether they are working on "time," or on "task work," no slacking can be allowed. The men in the fighting line depend on the men of the Labour Corps to keep them supplied with all they require.

### 5. *Working under Fire.*

The decision as to whether Labour Companies are to be put on work in a dangerous area rests with the G.O.C. Formation, or his local representative, and will depend largely on whether the work is of an urgent nature or not.

The decision to stop work owing to a locality being shelled or bombed will depend on the nature of the orders given to the officer in charge of the working party.

The senior combatant officer present would make the decision pending a reference to higher authority.

Occurrences of this kind will be reported on A.F. W. 3438.

In case it should be necessary to cease work owing to shelling or bombing, the Officer i/c Working Party should order his men to move to a place upon which he has previously decided until the shelling or bombing ceases.

Officers in such circumstances have a double duty. They must look after the safety of their men, and they must see that the work is done, if it is possible.

It is essential, therefore, that they learn how to keep their men under control, and the men must be trained to rally, after dispersal. It is advisable to select a rallying point on arrival at the place of work, if possible, far enough away to avoid shelling and yet near enough to see when work can be resumed.

A well trained company which has been practised in the above will have fewer casualties, and will do more work than a company not so trained.

There are no restrictions as to the areas where British labour companies may be employed, but it is to be remembered that the majority of the personnel are unarmed and untrained ; it is therefore necessary that Labour Companies should not be placed where they might be required to fight.

### 6. *Burial Parties.*

Divisions are primarily responsible for carrying out the burial of their own dead. But occasions may arise when Labour Companies are detailed to furnish burial parties near the fighting line.

Officers in charge of parties so detailed should ask for a guide to show them the route to the place where the work must be carried out, in order to avoid the risk of unnecessarily exposing their men, or of drawing fire on the fighting troops in the vicinity.

When Labour Companies have to undertake this work, it is important that they should not be kept too long at it. The best results are obtainable when a system of reliefs by units is organised, companies not being retained on the work for spells exceeding 4 days at a time, or a week at the most.

### 7. *Periods of Rest.*

Regular periods of rest should be arranged, without which it is impossible to keep men fit and to prevent staleness.

Experience has shown that labour is most economically used if work is continuous, *i.e.*, organised on the basis of seven full days' work a week, while each man has one day's rest in seven. If 15 per cent. of the men are rested at a time, this will enable each man to have one day's rest in seven.

But it depends entirely on the exigencies of the Service whether this can be carried out. One Employer may require Labour on six days only, if it is necessary for him to rest the whole of his supervising personnel on one day, while another will require Labour every day of the week. An example of the former is the C.R.E., and of the latter the Docks Directorate. As far as possible, definite units should be rested at a time, *i.e.*, companies, half-companies or platoons.

Men resting should not be put on fatigues or paraded more than absolutely necessary for carrying out inspections of clothing, gas appliances, &c.

It should be made quite clear to the men that in times of stress they will be called upon to perform seven full days' work a week.

In addition to the periodical rest of personnel, considerable benefit will result if arrangements can be made to relieve, periodically, the Labour Companies which are employed in the forward zones of Armies by units employed further back. A certain dislocation of work will result, but it is considered that the opportunity of giving tired companies better rest at night and a change from the more trying conditions of the forward Areas, will be for the benefit of the Labour Corps as a whole, and indirectly of the Army which they serve.

Care must however, be taken to warn the Employers of Labour before any reliefs of this nature are effected.

## CHAPTER III.—THE LABOUR GROUP.

1. The War Establishment of a Labour Group is as follows :—

| Detail. | Personnel. | | | | | Horses. | | | Bicycles. | Maltese cart. | Motor car. |
|---|---|---|---|---|---|---|---|---|---|---|---|
| | Officers. | Warrant officers. | Staff-serjeants and serjeants. | Rank and file. | Total. | Riding. | Draught. | Total. | | | |
| Lieut-colonel ... ... | 1 | ... | ... | ... | 1 | 1 | ... | 1 | ... | ... | 1e |
| Adjutant ... ... | 1 | ... | ... | ... | 1 | ... | ... | ... | 1 | ... | ... |
| Quartermaster ... ... | 1 | ... | ... | ... | 1 | ... | ... | ... | ... | ... | ... |
| Quartermaster-serjeant | ... | 1 | ... | ... | 1 | ... | ... | ... | ... | ... | ... |
| Orderly room serjeant... | ... | ... | 1 | ... | 1 | ... | ... | ... | ... | ... | ... |
| Clerks .. ... ... | ... | ... | ... | 2a | 2 | ... | ... | ... | ... | ... | ... |
| Other ranks ... | ... | ... | ... | 4b | 4 | ... | ... | ... | ... | ... | ...e |
| Orderlies for M.O. ... | ... | ... | ... | 2c | 2 | ... | ... | ... | ... | ... | ... |
| Batmen ... ... | ... | ... | ... | 4 | 4 | ... | ... | ... | ... | ... | ... |
| Total, excluding attached ... | 3 | 1 | 1 | 12 | 17 | 1 | ... | 1 | 1 | ... | 1 |
| *Attached—* | | | | | | | | | | | |
| Medical officer ... | 1 | ... | ... | ... | 1 | ... | ... | ... | ... | ... | ... |
| Drivers, A.S.C.— | | | | | | | | | | | |
| For vehicle ... | ... | ... | ... | (d) | ... | ... | 1 | 1 | ... | 1 | ... |
| For motor car ... | ... | ... | ... | 1e | 1 | ... | ... | ... | ... | ... | ... |
| Total, including attached ... | 4 | 1 | 1 | 13 | 19 | 1 | 1 | 2 | 1 | 1 | 1 |

(a) Includes a corporal.

(b) Includes a lance-corporal.

(c) Two men (one a lance-corporal), trained to the duties, are placed under the orders of the medical officer. The private drives the cart for medical equipment.

(d) Medical officer's orderly.

(e) One motor car is allowed in cases where the G.O.C. Formation considers such an issue necessary.

Note.—Where a Group contains any Labour companies other than British, one interpreter clerk for each nationality will be added to the Group Headquarters.

## 2. *Discipline.*

The Group Commander is the channel of communication between the Company Commander on the one hand and the Labour Commandant in Army Areas, the Base, or Administrative Commandant in the L. of C. Area.

The Group Commander should be personally acquainted with all officers in his Group, and should be able to give an opinion as to their respective capabilities. The Group Commander will forward to A.G.M.2 G.H.Q. direct on the first day of each month a nominal roll of all Officers under his Command.

The Group Commander should carefully watch the percentage of non-effectives in the companies under his administration.

The Group Commander is responsible that the current orders, governing the combing out of " A " men, are observed within his Group, and in particular will see that his Company Commanders keep lists of potential " A " men and ensure that the periodical medical examinations are made.

The Group Commander is responsible that his Adjutant studies all general and other routine orders, circular memoranda, standing orders, &c., as circulated to Labour Group Headquarters, and calls the attention of Company Commanders to those of importance and special interest.

The Group Commander, in addition to his Administrative and executive functions in connection with discipline and interior economy, is also responsible for the efficiency of the work performed by the Units in his Group.

He should constantly visit the Units at work, make himself thoroughly acquainted with the special aptitude of each Company, and ensure that the Company Officers are with their men at work.

He should ascertain by comparison between Units and from the Employers whether the output is satisfactory.

The Group Commander should take every opportunity of seeing that task work is introduced whenever possible, but care must be taken that the tasks set should not be too low. A scale should only be laid down after very careful observation and inquiry.

## 3. *Movements.*

On a unit marching in, the Group Commander is responsible :—

    (i) That an officer, or representative, of the Labour Group Headquarters meets the unit on arrival to point out selected site for camp and to give all information as to water supply, rations, ordnance, maps, &c., and location of nearest Divisional and Brigade H.Q.

    (ii) That the marching-in-state, showing strength of officers and O.R., details of transport, map reference, time of arrival, &c., is reported forthwith to the Labour Commandant or to Base or Area Headquarters.

(iii) That arrangements are made in advance to ration the incoming unit. Indents should, if necessary, be sent in by the Group Commander on the basis of a company at War Establishment.

On a unit marching out, the Group Commander is responsible :—

(i) That an advance party, under an officer, is detailed if possible.

(ii) That the necessary instructions are issued to all concerned, that the C.O. has a map and the most suitable route is chosen.

(iii) That an officer of the Labour Group Headquarters is present when the unit marches out, and the site is left clean.

(iv) That the marching-out-state and time of departure are notified forthwith to the Labour Commandant or to Base or Area Headquarters.

(v) That on the move of a company from his Group, any orders issued as to the number of days' rations to be carried are complied with. If no such orders are issued the Group Commander will issue orders that the company should carry rations up to and for the day following the day of arrival.

The personnel of Labour Companies is composed entirely of unfit men—many of them of advanced middle age—and consequently unable to march any considerable distance. 'Buses, or lorries, should therefore be applied for when necessary to Headquarters Formation concerned.

This particularly applies to arrivals of Labour Companies on detrainment in their new area. If the distance from the de-training station to the billet exceeds (say) five miles, application should invariably be made for 'buses, or alternately for lorries,—for the men and kit—or for kits only.

If a unit has no transport of its own, and is about to move, the O.C. Group will communicate with the Labour Commandant of the Army or the Corps or with the Headquarters of the Base or Administrative Area on the L. of C., who will make the necessary arrangements.

#### 4. *Accommodation, &c.*

The Group Quartermaster is responsible to the Group Commander for the billeting accommodation of the units in the Group.

The Labour Camps should be visited frequently by the Group Commander.

The condition of the huts or tents should be carefully watched —huts being kept water-tight and in good repair ; tents which become worn beyond local repair should be changed for others. Every Camp should have a small drying shed for clothes ; in many cases this can be heated from the incinerator. The sites on which

Camps are built should be changed when necessary, but this can only be done after obtaining the sanction of the Formation or Administrative Commandant.

The construction of latrines and urinals requires special attention and only in very rare cases will any difficulty be found in securing the advice and assistance of an expert from a neighbouring Sanitary unit.

In all areas information is available at the Headquarters of the Formations as to the fitness for drinking, or otherwise, of the various water supplies. A Group Commander should obtain this information directly he moves into an area—pass it on to Os.C. Companies, and take steps that the orders on this important point are strictly observed.

The question of good drinking water and the cleanliness of the water carts should have the particular attention of the Group M.O.

In practically every Formation there are arrangements for bathing, and it only remains for the O.C. Group to see that an allotment is made to the Labour Companies so that every man bathes regularly at least once a week. If, however, such baths are not available Companies must make their own bathing arrangements, unless the Group is sufficiently concentrated to allow units to use baths centrally situated. Group Commanders will decide which arrangement is to be adopted.

The Group Commander should acquaint himself with the laundry arrangements of the Formation to which he belongs, and take steps to ensure that all men within his administration have a sufficiency of clean underwear and socks.

Much can be done by a Group Commander in organising concerts and entertainments for the men and assisting Company Commanders to run Company Canteens if there are no others available. Inter-group and inter-company football can also be organised and every effort should be made to provide recreation for the men, so far as the circumstances will allow.

## 5. *Rations and Cooking.*

In this matter Labour Companies often require help. The Group Quartermaster, acting on the orders of the Group Commander, should visit the Companies regularly and frequently, examine the rations as drawn, and satisfy himself as to their quality and quantity. He should advise as to the best use to be made of the rations and their partition into the several meals, and should realise that on these points the Labour Companies to a large extent depend upon his expert advice for their comfort and good feeding. Field kitchens with ovens should be constructed to enable the meat to be sometimes roasted.

Arrangements should exist in every Labour Camp for the

provision of hot soup or tea for working parties returning to camp during the night or in the early hours of the morning.

Soyer stoves should be applied for where necessary (G.R.O. 1133).

It is very desirable that the Company Corporal Cook and as many assistants as possible should attend a course of instruction at the Army, Corps or Area Cookery School.

Attention is drawn to SS. 615 " Cooking in the Field," which gives full information on the preparation of diet sheets and recipes.

It will be possible in some cases for the supplies of all the units in the Group to be drawn as a whole by the Group Quartermaster. This will result in a saving of transport, and close supervision by the Group Headquarters of the supplies issued will probably result in better messing.

If, however, this cannot be arranged, the Quartermaster should visit the refilling points and see that the Labour Companies receive their due supplies, fuel, forage, &c.

### 6. *Ordnance Stores.*

It is generally advisable that indents for ordnance stores be passed through the Labour Group Headquarters for information and scrutiny.

In certain cases where the companies in a Group are located near each other and draw from the same Ordnance Store, it may be possible for the Group Quartermaster to draw the Ordnance stores for the entire Group and distribute to the units.

This would save transport.

To ensure that the men of Labour Companies are properly clothed and equipped, periodical inspections by the Group Commander or by the Group Quartermaster, acting under the former's orders, are desirable.

Boots require special attention and care should be taken by Platoon Commanders not only to see that boots are in good repair, but that the men are issued with boots of proper size.

There is a general tendency in units to accumulate unauthorised and unnecessary stores. This should be watched and prevented.

### 7. *Transport.*

Company transport should be inspected at intervals by the Group Commander, or by an officer of his H.Q. detailed by him.

Horse standings should be kept in good repair, and overhead cover and protection from the prevailing winds provided.

In cases where a unit cannot draw its supplies, application should be made for the supplies to be delivered to the Camp by the Supply Column concerned.

The pooling of the Company Transport in a Group Area may, in some cases, be found to be economical, but this of course depends on the geographical situation of the units in the Group.

When a unit moves from one area to another it will not necessarily retain its transport. The conditions under which it will be working in the new area will determine what transport, if any, it will take with it. The O.C. Group will obtain instructions from his Labour Commandant before issuing instructions for the move of any transport.

### 8. *General Administration.*

Frequent cases occur when men, through ignorance, look up and do not keep still when enemy aircraft are passing over, and the result may be that the locality is shelled. Instructions on this point are issued by the staffs of Formations and the Group Commander is responsible that the Standing Orders are promulgated to companies and made known to every man.

Group Commanders in Army Areas are responsible that all officers and men in their Groups are instructed in the use of anti-gas appliances and properly equipped in this respect. This matter is one which requires frequent inspections by specially trained N.C.Os. or men.

The fullest advantage should be taken of Army Corps and Divisional Anti-Gas Schools where courses of Instruction are held. At least two officers and four N.C.Os. per company should have gone through a course of anti-gas instruction.

Cases occur when a company is in a more or less isolated position and cannot be seen daily by the M.O. attached to the Group Headquarters. It is then the duty of the Labour Commandant to arrange for medical attendance in some other way by application to the Senior Medical Officer of the Formation by which the Group is administered.

The senior Veterinary Officer of the Formation concerned will arrange for the necessary veterinary services, on application being made to him. Group Commanders should obtain copies of " Animal Management."

### 9. *Responsibility of Company Commanders.*

It must be remembered that Labour Companies are self-accounting units and that the Company Commander normally has the powers of a Commanding Officer.

Nothing in the above is intended to relieve, in any degree, the responsibilities of an O.C. Labour Company.

### 10. *Companies divided between Group Areas.*

Occasions may arise where Labour Companies have personnel in more than one area. In such a case where a unit in one Group Area has a portion *detached* in another Group Area, the latter Group Headquarters should administer the detachment ; but where a Company whose Headquarters is in one Group Area merely overflows, by the spreading of its work, into another Group Area, then the Labour Group Headquarters in whose area the headquarters of the Company is located, should continue to administer the whole Company.

### CHAPTER IV.—THE LABOUR COMPANY.

1. The following notes apply to all labour. Special Notes applying to the various nationalities represented in the Labour Corps are to be found in later chapters.

The war establishment of a British Labour Company consists of a Headquarters and four Platoons. The company is commanded by a Major or Captain, and a platoon by a Subaltern Officer.

A platoon consists of two sections, each under a Sergeant.

A section consists of two subsections, each under a corporal.

| Detail. | Personnel. | | | | | Horses. | | | | Bicycles. |
|---|---|---|---|---|---|---|---|---|---|---|
| | Officers. | Warrant officers. | Staff-serjeants and serjeants. | Rank and file. | Total. | Riding. | Draught. | Heavy draught. | Total. | |
| Major or captain ... | 1 | ... | ... | ... | 1 | (a) | ... | ... | ... | (a) |
| Subalterns ... ... | 4 | ... | ... | ... | 4 | ... | ... | ... | ... | 2 |
| Company serjeant-major | ... | 1 | ... | ... | 1 | ... | ... | ... | ... | ... |
| Company Q.M. serjeant | ... | ... | 1 | ... | 1 | ... | ... | ... | ... | ... |
| Serjeants ... ... | ... | ... | 8 | ... | 8 | ... | ... | ... | ... | ... |
| Corporals (b) ... ... | ... | ... | ... | 18 | 18 | ... | ... | ... | ... | ... |
| Privates (c) ... ... | ... | ... | ... | 461 | 461 | ... | ... | ... | ... | ... |
| Batmen ... ... ... | ... | ... | ... | 6 | 6 | ... | ... | ... | ... | ... |
| Total (excluding attached)... ... | 5 | 1 | 9 | 485 | 500 | ... | ... | ... | ... | 2 |
| *Attached—* | | | | | | | | | | |
| Medical officer (d) ... | 1 | ... | ... | ... | 1 | ... | ... | ... | ... | ... |
| Drivers, A.S.C.— | | | | | | | | | | |
| For vehicles ... | ... | ... | ... | 4e | 4 | ... | 4 | 4 | 8 | — |
| For spare horse ... | ... | ... | ... | 1 | 1 | ... | 1 | ... | 1 | ... |
| Spare ... ... | ... | ... | ... | 1 | 1· | ... | ... | ... | ... | ... |
| Drivers, A.S.C. (second line transport) ... | ... | ... | ... | 2 | 2 | ... | ... | 4 | 4 | ... |
| Total (including attached)... ... | 6 | 1 | 9 | 493 | 509 | (a) | 5 | 8 | 13 | 2 |

(a) One riding horse, or a bicycle, will be allowed for the O.C. when considered necessary by G.O.C. Formation.

(b) Includes 1 corporal cook and 1 corporal clerk.

(c) Includes 6 lance-corporals, 2 men trained in sanitary duties, cooks and artificers.

(d) Two men from the company (1 lance-corporal), trained to the duties, are placed under the orders of the M.O. The private drives the cart for medical equipment. The M.O. will not be attached when the company is administered by a Group Headquarters.            (e) Includes a corporal.

## 2. *Discipline.*

The Company Commander is responsible to the O.C. Group Headquarters to which he is attached for the discipline and general efficiency of his Company. On arrival in an Area an officer in command of, or appointed to command, a Labour Company will report to the Group Commander. Other Company Officers will report to the O.C. Company.

The Company Commander is responsible for detailing working parties, &c., in accordance with the instruction for allotment issued to him by the Group Commander.

He is responsible that his men are not detailed for " Employments" (*i.e.*, work which should be performed by men of Area Employment Companies) without orders in writing from his Group Commander authorising such employment.

He must see that his officers do not carry out duties apart from their units, and that they render every assistance to the Employer in carrying out the work for which their men are detailed.

The powers of a Company Commander vary with the different types of labour which they command and are dealt with in the notes on each type of labour.

The Company Commander should inspect his working parties at least once a day. There is sometimes a tendency on the part of Company Commanders to remain in Camp and not get about sufficiently. If a Company is properly organised and administered, the routine work should not occupy the C.O. more than two or three hours per day.

The efficiency of a Company depends more than anything else on the spirit of the men, and this in its turn depends to a large extent on the officers and N.C.Os. The officers and N.C.Os. should make a point of attending to the comfort of their men before their own, and seeing that, as far as possible, their billets are made comfortable, and their food is regularly received and properly cooked.

By close co-operation with the Employer under whose instructions they are working, and with the Group Commander to which they are attached, much trouble can be avoided.

During the short time the Labour Corps has been in existence an *esprit de corps* has been created, and its work is often carried out under conditions which call for a high degree of endurance and courage.

To attain this, however, it is essential that discipline should be good. By good discipline is meant not only immediate obedience to verbal orders while at work, or in camp, but what is just as important, a strict observance of all orders as to frequenting estaminets, censorship, and other matters, especially sanitation and cleanliness. All such orders are issued with one object only—to increase the efficiency of the Army as a fighting machine.

A corps or regiment is, to a great extent, judged by the way in which its personnel conduct themselves in public. Special attention should, therefore, be paid by all ranks to saluting. The saluting of senior officers by junior officers and other ranks is to be strictly observed, and officers must invariably return the salutes of all ranks whether British or Allied, in the proper manner (see G.R.Os. 81, 1736 and 2635). The attention of all ranks should be drawn to the orders as to saluting General Officers in motor cars, *i.e.*, those bearing flags.

Simple squad drill should be practised so that parties marching to and from work shall do so smartly and in proper formation. Officers and N.C.Os. will be careful to call parties to attention and pay compliments on the march when necessary. Slack march discipline should not be permitted. An N.C.O. should always march in the rear of a party, even though he is the only N.C.O. with the party.

It is extremely important for officers to set an example of energy and keenness, and to take a personal interest in the welfare, discipline and comfort of the men under their command.

### 3. *Care of the Men.*

Company Commanders should see that their men's feet are regularly inspected, especially during severe weather, and should ensure that cases of sore heels, blisters, &c., are attended to. A strapping of soap plaster placed over a blister with some boracic powder placed in the sock often enables a man to " carry on." The wearing of a second pair of socks is found of great assistance by some men.

The maintenance of a high standard of cleanliness in camp, is essential. *The disposal of refuse*, the cleanliness of cook-houses and billets, and the construction of proper stores for meat and other food should receive constant attention.

These matters of comfort, feeding, and sanitation have a most important effect upon the health and available strength of the company and the work done by it.

All Officers are personally responsible that the orders and instructions from time to time issued on the subject of hygiene are carried out in every detail. As the method of treatment of such matters as frostbite is continually being improved, it is not thought advisable to include any notes upon the subject in this publication.

Attention is, however, particularly drawn to G.R.O. 127t (in Part I, Extracts) and every Officer must make himself acquainted with all amendments of the above and all orders published by Formations on the subject.

Os.C. Companies are responsible for the provision of proper latrine accommodation for working parties, and that trench latrines are properly filled in when the work is finished. Disciplinary action should be taken against any man neglecting to use such latrines.

When men are constantly at work of the kind that is done by the Labour Corps, they are apt to get slack as regards cleanliness of person as well as of clothing. This cannot in any circumstances be permitted.

Os.C. Companies must hold Platoon Commanders responsible for the cleanliness of their men, that their hair is cut, and that their clothes are kept clean and tidy.

It should be a standing order in every Company that, except when men are proceeding to or from work, they should not leave camp or billet without reporting at the Guard room and being inspected. Men on pass will invariably wear belts and puttees.

Parties should always be inspected on parade before marching off.

When at work men should take their coats off if the weather is suitable.

#### 4. C'othing and Equipment.

The scale of clothing for a labour company is the same as that for Infantry (see Extracts G.R.O's. Part II.), with the following additions :—

    (a) 1 suit of worn clothing for working clothes.

    (b) 1 pair of worn boots and laces.

    (c) Kitbag.

    (d) Oilskins and sou'westers.

For Equipment, see Mobilization Store Table A.F.G. 1098-334.

A Company Commander is not absolved of his responsibility for the proper clothing and equipping of his Company merely by rendering indents. If they are not complied with in a reasonable time he must refer the matter to Group Headquarters.

#### 5. Care of Animals.

The O.C. Company is responsible for the care of the horses and vehicles allotted to his unit. It is, therefore, essential that he and his subaltern officers should make themselves acquainted with at least the elements of horse-mastership and transport maintenance. Some instructions as to the care of horses and mules will be found in Chapter XII. A pamphlet on "Horse Management in the Field" can be obtained from Publications, Boulogne.

### 6. *The Platoon Commander.*

The Platoon Commander is responsible to the O.C. of his Company for the efficiency and well-being of the men in his platoon. Certain powers of punishment may be delegated to him by the O.C. Company to assist him to maintain discipline in his platoon, but Os.C. Companies will always satisfy themselves that Platoon Commanders have sufficient experience to justify their being entrusted with these powers.

The Platoon Commander will be with his platoon from the time it parades for duty till it has been dismissed on return to camp, unless detailed for or given permission to attend to, other duties by the O.C. Company.

Platoon Commanders will make themselves acquainted as far as possible with the duties of an O.C. Company, in order to fit themselves to take command of a company or detachment, if required. They should attend at the Company Orderly Room from time to time and become familiar with orderly room procedure as well as conversant with King's Regulations, the Army Act, and regimental work generally.

While Platoon Commanders are responsible for supervising the work of the men under them, they will work under the orders of the representative of the Service, or Directorate, by whom the labour is being employed, whatever the rank or seniority of this officer. It is the duty of the Platoon Commander to see that his men carry out efficiently and quickly the work required by this officer.

It is the duty of the Platoon commander to see, when the weather is doubtful, that the men are carrying their oilskins, and, if they are not returning to billets for the mid-day meal, that a proper haversack ration is provided, in addition to seeing that they have a good breakfast before they start.

### 7. *Regimental Employ.*

It is imperative that the maximum amount of productive work should be obtained from every labourer, white or coloured.

Os.C. Companies and Platoons must use every effort to ensure that as large a proportion of their men as possible are actually available for work. This can be secured by doing everything to reduce the number of men on regimental employ, and arranging that Servants' Guard, Orderly, Sanitary and Camp duties generally, are performed, as far as possible, by men unfitted for more active work.

The following instructions issued by one of the Armies are a guide on the subject :—

NUMBERS OF ALL RANKS WHO ARE TO BE CONSIDERED AS AUTHORISED REGIMENTAL EMPLOYMENTS.

| — | C.S.M. | C.Q.M.S. | Clerk. | Police. | Postman. | Storeman. | Shoemakers. | Barber. | Tailor. | Batmen. | Sanitary Men. | Runner. | Cooks. | Total. |
|---|---|---|---|---|---|---|---|---|---|---|---|---|---|---|
| H.Q. and 4 Platoons. | 1 | 1 | 1 | 2 | 1 | 1 | 2 | 1 | 1 | 3 | 2 | 1 | 5 | 22 |
| H.Q. and 1 Platoon. | 1 | 1 | 1 | 1 | 1 | 1 | 2 | 1 | 1 | 2 | 1 | 1 | 2 | 16 |
| H.Q. and 2 Platoons. | 1 | 1 | 1 | 1 | 1 | 1 | 2 | 1 | 1 | 2 | 1 | 1 | 3 | 17 |
| H.Q. and 3 Platoons. | 1 | 1 | 1 | 1 | 1 | 1 | 2 | 1 | 1 | 3 | 2 | 1 | 4 | 20 |
| 2 Platoons on Detachment. | — | — | 1 | — | — | — | — | — | — | 1 | 1 | 1 | 3 | 7 |
| 1 Platoon on Detachment. | — | — | 1 | — | — | — | — | — | — | 1 | 1 | 1 | 2 | 6 |

NOTE.

*Batmen.*—To be used all day in orderly duties about camp.

*Police.*—Number will vary according to circumstances, but should in no case be more than two.

*Barber.*—When not working as a barber he will be employed on orderly duties in camp.

*Sanitary.*—Additional men for any other regimental duties must be furnished from Light Duty men.

Men chosen to fill the above employments, subject to their being suitable, should be from Light Duty men wherever possible.

The Sick Corporal is not shown as Company Employ, as on returning from Sick Parade he should take the M. & D. men to the working party and rejoin his platoon.

There will be an Orderly Corporal for the day, or for the week, as the case may be. He will not stay in camp, but will accompany his working party.

## 8. *Fire Precautions.*

Company Commanders are responsible that all precautions are observed against Fire (see G.R.Os. 2717, 4447 and the chapter on Fire Precautions in G.R.O. Extracts, Part II). Fire orders must be posted in all billets and huts.

# CHAPTER V.—ORDERS, BOOKS, RETURNS, &c.

1. Every Group and Company Headquarters should receive copies of all G.R.Os. as they are issued through Publications, Boulogne.

Group Commanders are responsible that the units under their command receive copies of R.O.s of the Army, L. of C. or Formation, by which they are administered. The standing orders of such Formations should also be obtained and circulated.

Company Officers must be particularly careful that all Orders are duly promulgated, any special Order affecting Labour should be re-embodied in Company Orders, which should always be read out on parade and thereafter posted up.

### 2. *Books, &c., to be kept in a Labour Company.*

By the O.C. Company :—

Nominal Roll of the whole Company;
Cash Book;
Acquittance Rolls, A.F. N. 1513A;
A copy of the Mobilisation Store Table of his Unit;
Ration Indents A.B. 55;
Ordnance Indents A.F. G. 994;
R.E. Stores Indents A.B. F. 30;
Cooking in the Field;
S.S. 571, Ration pamphlet;
Camp Equipment and Stores Book, recording receipts and issues with dates. A.B. 129 may be used;
Defaulter Book, A.B. 2069;
Billeting Book, A.B. 397;
Billeting Distribution List, A.F. W. 3401;
A.F. B. 122 (Conduct sheets). The method of keeping these is fully explained in the book;
King's Regulations;
Manual of Military Law;
Field Service Regulations, Parts I and II;
Extracts from G.R.Os., Parts I and II (S.S. 309 and S.S. 340);
Royal Warrant for Pay and Allowances;
Allowance Regulations;
F.S. Pocket Book.

All the above are obtainable on indent on the Army Printing and Stationery Depôt.

A Field Service Stationery box is supplied (empty) by the A.O.D. on indent.

Great care must be exercised in keeping the records of the company, which can best be done by filing a copy of the casualties reported weekly on A.F. B. 213 together with the Company Orders.

Immediately a N.C.O. or man becomes non-effective by death or transfer to England his Field Conduct Sheet, A.F. B. 122, should be dispatched to the Officer in charge of Labour Corps Section, 3rd Echelon.

By Platoon Commanders and Officers in Charge of Detachments :—

Squad Book, which must show the following particulars :—

Regimental No., Rank, Names in full, date and place of enlistment, name and address of next of kin, religion, trade or calling in civil life, dates of inoculation and vaccination, previous service and date of discharge, casualties affecting a man's rank or pay.

(If the height and boot sizes are recorded, it is of great assistance to Quartermasters when indenting for fresh clothing.)

Names are to be arranged in alphabetical order.

On handing over from one Platoon Officer to another a receipt should be given on the first page of the book ; this page will also clearly record the different Platoon Commanders' names and periods of command.

A Squad Book is published by Gale and Polden, Aldershot, and other Army publishers.

The O.C. Company will frequently inspect the Squad Books.

When on detachment the officer in charge of detachment will keep conduct sheets, A.F. B. 122, of the men under him.

### 3. *Returns to be Rendered.*

By Platoon Commanders.—A.F. W. 3438 (Work Report), daily, to O.C. Company.

By Company Commanders.—A.F. W. 3439 (Return of Labour and Strength Return), daily, to O.C. Group H.Q. and Labour Commandant (or Assistant Controller if on the L. of C.).

When Unit moves, marching in and out state and disposal of transport should be sent to O.C., Group H.Q. (see Form of Return in Appendix " A.").

By Group Commanders.—*A.F. W. 3719 (Marching in and out state), when unit moves, to Labour Command nt (or Assistant Controller if on the L. of C.).

### By Labour Commandant, Corps H.Q.

| No. of Form. | When rendered. | To whom rendered. | Nature of return. |
|---|---|---|---|
| *A.F. W. 3719 ... | When unit moves | Labour Commandant, Army H.Q. | Marching in and out state. |
| L. 11 ... | Weekly ... | Labour Commandant, Army H.Q. | Distribution and allocation of labour. |

## By Assistant Controller on L. of C.

| No. of Form. | When rendered. | To whom rendered. | Nature of return. |
|---|---|---|---|
| A.F.W. 3718 | ... Weekly ... | ... Deputy Controller... | Labour used on tonnage (in duplicate). |
| A.F.W. 3720 | ... Weekly ... | ... Deputy Controller... | Distribution and allocation of labour. |
| *A.F.W. 3719 | ... When unit moves | Deputy Controller... | Marching in and out state. |

## By Labour Commandant, Army H.Q. in Army Area.

| No. of Form. | When rendered. | To whom rendered. | Nature of return. |
|---|---|---|---|
| L. 11.  ... | ... Weekly ... | ... Controller of Labour | Distribution and allocation of labour. |
| *A.F.W. 3719 | ... When unit moves | Controller of Labour | Marching in and out state. |
| A.F.W. 3721 | ... Weekly ... | ... Controller of Labour | Labour forecast. |

## By Deputy Controllers, L. of C. Area.

| No. of Form. | When rendered. | To whom rendered. | Nature of return. |
|---|---|---|---|
| A.F.W. 3720 | ... Weekly ... | ... Controller of Labour | Distribution and allocation of labour. |
| A.F.W. 3721 | ... Weekly ... | ... H.Q. L. of C. Area | Labour forecast. |
| A.F.W. 3718 | ... Weekly ... | ... Controller of Labour | Labour used on tonnage. |
| A.F.W. 3719 | ... When unit moves | Controller of Labour and H.Q. L. of C. Area. | Marching in and out state. |

* Marching-in-states, should be sent in by D.R.L.S., and should include, in addition to the numbers of personnel and transport, the location of the unit either by reference to a place or by map reference.

By Labour Commandants and Deputy Controllers.—A.F.C. 2118 War Diary in Duplicate), monthly, to D.A.G. 3rd Echelon.

Great stress is laid on the correct filling up of A.Fs. W. 3438 and 3439. Company Commanders must see that A.F. W. 3438 is properly filled in by the Officer, or N.C.O. in charge of each party, and that the information in column 7 of that form is embodied in A.F. W. 3439, or on a slip attached to it.

Other returns will, of course, be rendered as called for by formations.

## CHAPTER VI.—CASUALTIES.

1. Officers Commanding Labour Group Headquarters will report all " casualties " affecting officers, *e.g.*, admission to, or discharge from, hospital, arrivals and departures, by D.R.L.S. to A.G. M. 2, General Headquarters. All applications for Officers will be made to the same branch.

Under "Casualties " the following are included —

    (i) Deaths.
    (ii) Promotions and reductions.
    (iii) Transfers.
    (iv) Leaves.
    (v) Absence without leave.
    (vi) Reinforcements.
    (vii) Self-inflicted and accidental injuries.
    (viii) Evacuation to hospital.
    (ix) Admission to prison.
    (x) Casualties in soldier's family.

Whether affecting officers or O.R., all such " casualties " will be reported weekly to D.A.G., 3rd Echelon, on A.F. B. 213 and as may otherwise be ordered by the Formation. Attention is drawn to G.R.O. **3867**. The information given in F.S. Regulations Part II, Chap. XVI, pp. 162 to 178, should be taken as a general guide.

Deaths will only be reported by the Commander of the Unit if the soldier is not in medical charge.

### 2. *Promotions and Reductions.*

If a N.C.O. is evacuated to hospital, transferred, reduced or dies the Company Commander may appoint another N C.O. to acting rank to complete Establishment. All appointments will be referred through Group Headquarters to D.A.G. for confirmation. They will date from the day after the vacancy and, after being confirmed, will appear in A.F. B. 213 ; the necessary entries will also be made in A.B. 64.

All appointments, whether paid or unpaid, must appear on A.F. B. 213, and it must be shown clearly whether they are " paid " or " unpaid." Particular attention is drawn to G.R.O. 2202.

Os.C. Companies must be most careful not to exceed the authorised Establishment of N.C.Os.

Example for A.F.B. 213 : A/Cpl. Smith, J., deprived of A/Rank 31/8/15. Replaced by Pte. Jones, T., appointed A/Cpl. 1/9/15 with (or without) pay.

The following is an extract from A.C.I. 1013 :—

As there are a number of supernumerary substantive warrant officers and colour serjeants (or corresponding ranks) in other corps, no promotion of N.C.Os. in the Labour Corps to the above ranks will be made until the supernumeraries have been absorbed by transfer to the Labour Corps.

Appointments to acting serjeant-major, acting regimental quartermaster-serjeant, acting company serjeant-major and acting company quartermaster-serjeant may be made provisionally by Os.C. Units both abroad and at home pending notification from the Officer i/c Labour Corps Records as to how the vacancy is to be filled.

In order to enable the Officer i/c Labour Corps Records to fill the appointments of company quartermaster-serjeant with the best men available, Os.C. Labour Corps Units will notify from time to time the names of N.C.Os. on the strength of their units who are recommended for such promotion.

In the case of units serving abroad the names will be submitted to the O.C. Labour Group Headquarters or an Officer not below the rank of lieutenant-colonel who will countersign the recommendation if he considers it justified and forward it direct to the Officer i/c Labour Corps Records. He will inform the O.C. unit concerned in writing of the names of any N.C.Os. whom he does not consider suitable for promotion, and their names will not be passed to the Officer i/c Records.

The names of all N.C.Os. recommended for promotion to company quartermaster-serjeant will be placed on a general corps roster in order of seniority, and vacancies when necessary will be filled by the Officer i/c Labour Corps Records from this roster.

See also G.R.O. 4297.

### 3. *Reinforcements and Transfers.*

Full details of each soldier having been taken on the strength will be shown. Absentees rejoining their units or men returning from hospital will also be shown.

Transfers can only take place by order of superior authority, which must be quoted when the casualty is reported on A.F.B. 213.

### 4. *Leave.*

The period of leave should be stated (*see* G.R.O. 3348). A further entry will be made when the soldier rejoins, giving the date. If an extension has been granted the period of such extension and authority should be given.

In the case of a man being absent without leave, *after* he has been absent 21 clear days, a Court of Enquiry should be held, *see* paras. 514, 673 (as amended by A.O. 281 of 1917), and 1912 K.R. and Sect. 72 A.A. (*see also* G.R.O. 1379). If the Court declares the man to be a deserter, the fact is reported on A.F. B. 115, which is forwarded to Group Headquarters.

The Court of Enquiry must not be held until 21 complete days have passed (exclusive of the day on which the man went absent, and of the day on which the Court is assembled) since he went absent, otherwise the declaration will be valueless for all purposes. The proceedings of the Court of Enquiry should be forwarded to the Group Headquarters for transmission to the Base, together with A.F. B. 115 compiled strictly in accordance with G.R.O. 3653.

### 5. *Injuries, Admissions to Hospital.*

In case of admission to hospital the entry in A.B. 213 should state date and whether sick, wounded or accidentally injured.

For instructions regarding self-inflicted and accidental and other injuries, *see* G.R.Os. 2311, 3355, 3867 and A.F. W. 3428.

### 6. *Punishments.*

Field Punishment.—The punishment awarded should be entered, *e.g.*, 10 days F.P. No. 1.

Prison.—Men sentenced to terms of imprisonment (unless the sentence is suspended) are struck off the strength as from the date of leaving the unit (*see* G.R.O 3578, para. 2).

### 7. *Casualties in Soldiers' Families.*

It is of great assistance, from an accounting point of view, if any information affecting a man's family (*e.g.*, the birth of a child) is included on A.F. B. 213. The information should be in the following form :—

" No. 2057, Jones, A., Private. States child born 3.9.17."

This information is transmitted to England for corroboration, and facilitates the necessary increase in Separation Allowance and Allotment.

### 8. *Striking off Strength.*

Before reinforcements can be demanded, casualties must be struck off the strength of the unit. For instructions *see* G.R.O. 3578 as amended by G.R.O. 3765. Men on Command are not casualties and should not be struck off the strength.

### 9. *Reinforcements and Depots.*

Reinforcements are obtained—

(i) From Labour Centres in England ;
(ii) From officers and O.R. in France, who are classified as unfit for the front line.

All officers and O.R. from England are sent direct to the Labour Corps Base Depôt, Boulogne, and from there are drafted into companies. Officers and O.R. already transferred to the Labour Corps, are similarly dealt with on evacuation from hospital, &c.

Officers already in France, who are classified as unfit for the front line, and posted to the Labour Corps, are also sent to the Depôt at Boulogne.

O.R. in France classified as unfit for the front line, are despatched to Employment Base Depôts at Calais, Etaples, Havre, and Rouen, and in the case of Boulogne they are sent to the Labour Corps Base Depot (from these depôts they are posted to the Labour Corps Units). Men of technical units, and men employed by units and Departments within their establishments, will be absorbed by the units, or departments, and not transferred to the Labour Corps.

All applications for personnel of other ranks will be made to D.A.G., 3rd Echelon, on perforated sheet attached to A.F. B. 213.

## CHAPTER VII.—PAY.

1. The system of payment in the Labour Corps as regards British labour is the same as in other units of the Army.

N.C.Os. and men should be paid once a week (unless circumstances render this impracticable) and in multiples of 5 francs. Payments should never be made in excess of the credit shown in a man's Pay Book (A.B. 64).

Care must be taken not to overpay men who have made allotments.

The O.C. Company must open an Imprest Account with the Staff Paymaster i/c Clearing House, to whom he should apply for an Imprest Account number.

Cash is drawn on A.F. 3100, upon which the Imprest Holder gives his receipt for the cash issued. If unable to attend himself, he will give a written authority to another Officer to draw the cash on his behalf.

Cash must always be drawn by a Commissioned Officer. If an Officer holding an Imprest Account goes sick, the name of his substitute must be notified to the Staff Paymaster i/c Clearing House before any further cash can be drawn. This should be done through Group Headquarters. Imprest holders should be prepared to satisfy the Field Cashier as to their identity if required.

Attention is drawn to G.R.O. 1912 in Extracts from G.R.Os., Part I.

Only the amount of cash required for making payments should be drawn. Imprest holders are not to retain excessive balances.

A.F. N. 1513 should always be used when pay is issued. They must be made out in duplicate, one copy to be a carbon copy, and the signatures to be carbon copies of the signatures on the original. The duplicate is retained for two months and then sent to O. i/c

D.A.R. Deposit Store—A.P.O. S. 38—marked "Duplicate." (See G.R.Os. 1913 and 2615, Part I, Extracts G.R.Os. Men of different Units should be shown on separate rolls.

After pay has been issued the Acquittance Rolls should be completed as directed, and the original forwarded to Paymaster i/c Clearing House, with A.F. N. 1461A, showing the cash balance left in the hands of the Imprest Holder.

## 2. *The Soldier's Field Pay Book (A.B.*64).

See G.R.Os. in Extracts G.R.Os. Part I. A.B.64 should be in the possession of the man to whom it belongs ; he is responsible for the safe custody of the same. No man who is not in possession of his pay book may be paid. In the event of the loss of an A.B. 64, the instructions on page 1, para. 5 of A.B.64 must be at once complied with. The other instructions on page 1 should be carefully noted.

Entries on pages 2 and 3 should never be altered to show increase or decrease of pay or allotment ; any such alterations should be given in the columns provided for the purpose on pages 4 and 5, and cash columns.

Os.C. Companies must remember that they are personally responsible for any over-payments. Os.C. Companies can, if necessary, apply for a statement of a man's account to his Regimental Paymaster. In the case of men enrolled in, or transferred to, the Labour Corps, the Regimental Paymaster is at Eagle Works, Nottingham.

The net daily rate of pay, in page 4, is the rate of pay due to a man after deducting the amount of his allotment.

Casualties and punishments not affecting the *net* daily *rate* of pay should not be entered on page 5.

Every casualty which affects the amount of pay due to a man, *i.e.*, whether it affects his net daily rate of pay, or is only the stoppage of a certain number of days' pay, should be shown in the cash column ; the amount so forfeited must be shown as a cash payment, and will be calculated on the *gross* daily rate of pay. (Reference F.S.R., Part II., Chap. XV., Section 128, para. 10.)

The cash columns of A.B.64 require all entries to be made which affect the total amount due to a man at any time ; therefore remittances home should also appear in the cash column in *red ink.* In order to draw attention to amendments made in the net daily rate of pay, all promotions, reductions, and increases or decreases in allotments will be entered in the cash columns in *red ink.* Credits due to a man (*i.e.*, ration allowance during leave) should also be noted in cash columns.

Dates when a man goes on leave must be entered in his Pay Book. Local or acting ranks without pay should not be entered in the Pay Book.

In the A.B.64 recently issued there is a space for inserting the kit and necessaries issued to a man. For books in which this space is not allowed for, a form is issued, which, when filled in, can be pasted into the Book. Only the first issue either on coming abroad or when the Book is first made up, should be inserted.

The A.B.64 contains a short form of a Will, and advantage of this form should be taken by N.C.Os. and men.

An A.B.64 when finished with should be taken from the N.C.O. or man and sent to D.A.G. 3rd Echelon. Care must be taken to carry the total of the Cash Columns to the new book and if necessary to fill in the amount the soldier is in debt on page 6. All entries on pages 2, 3, 4, and 5 will be filled in from the old book.

The regimental number of a man transferred to the Labour Corps should be altered in his A.B. 64.

----

## CHAPTER VIII.—DISCIPLINE. PROCEDURE UNDER MILITARY LAW.

These notes are applicable to white labour, and in applying them to coloured labour, reference should be made to the special notes on the various nationalities of coloured labour.

An O.C. a Labour Company is a Commanding Officer, and, as such, can exercise the full powers of punishment which are laid down in para. 493 K.R., unless such powers are restricted by the O.C. a Labour Group.

G.R.O. 2472 states : The question of the disciplinary powers of Os.C. Labour Group Headquarters and of Os.C. Labour Companies has recently been under consideration.

1. An O.C. a Labour Group Headquarters is not a " superior authority" within the meaning of para. 487 K.R. Such superior authority is the Corps Commander in the case of Labour Groups working in Corps Areas, and the Area or Base Commandant in the case of Labour Groups working in L. of C. area.

2. An O.C. a Labour Company is a Commanding Officer, and as such can exercise the full powers of punishment which are laid down in para. 493 K.R. In view, however, of the fact that some of these officers have neither the seniority nor the experience which should be possessed by officers exercising these full powers, it is considered desirable that authority should be given to limit, when necessary, their prerogatives of punishment. The disciplinary powers of an O.C. a Labour Company may therefore be restricted at the discretion of the O.C. a Labour Group Headquarters to that of awarding 7 days in the case of F.P. No. 1 and No. 2, and for-feiture of pay under Section 46 (2) (d) A.A. In the case of

D 4

N.C.Os. such disciplinary power may be restricted to admonition of a N.C.O. of any rank, and to reprimand and severe reprimand of N.C.Os. of and under the rank of Corporal.

NOTE.—Detention is not awarded in France.

## 2. Offences.

As, however, crimes committed on Active Service assume a more serious aspect than similar crimes committed in England, Os. C. Companies should take the first opportunity of consulting O.C. Group Headquarters and obtain his advice as to the punishments which should be awarded.

For offences with which a Commanding Officer can deal summarily without reference to superior authority, but subject to such restriction as mentioned in para. I., see F.S.R. Part II., Chap. XIII., Section 106. For Forms of Charges see Appendix I, Rules of Procedure—Manual of Military Law, page 659.

Every charge against a soldier will be investigated without delay in his presence. Cases of soldiers in arrest will be disposed of daily. If a soldier is remanded and retained in arrest his case will be brought under review daily, in accordance with K.R. 485. A soldier in arrest should be interviewed once a day by an officer (see K.R. para., 484).

A Commanding Officer should dismiss any case in which after full investigation and hearing the evidence for the prosecution and defence he is *fully* satisfied that there is not sufficient evidence to support a charge ; but, in cases in which officers are involved, he should after investigation, refer the matter to the Group Commander.

If a C.O. proposes to deal with a case summarily *otherwise than by awarding a minor punishment* he must ask the soldier whether he desires to be dealt with summarily or to be tried by Court Martial.

If the soldier elects to be dealt with by his C.O. and is sentenced, he cannot afterwards claim a Court Martial. (*See also* Chap. IV., Sections (i), (ii) and (iii) Manual of Military Law.)

## 3. Minor Punishments.

K.R. 493 defines " minor punishments " as follows :—For private solders only, (a) C.B. up to 14 days (punishment drill as defined in K.R. 498, being permissible, during first 10 days) ; (b) Extra guards and piquets for offences on these duties ; (c) Admonition. *For N.C.Os. only*, (a) Severe reprimand ; (b) Reprimand ; (c) Admonition.

NOTE.—" C.B." is not applicable to Active Service. A man can, however, be " Confined to Camp."

An acting or lance N.C.O. may be ordered by a C.O. to revert to his permanent grade, but is not liable to summary or minor punishment in addition (K.R. para. 499).

K.R. 494 (vi) states that a defaulter is not required to undergo any punishment drill or C.B. which may have lapsed by reason of his being in hospital.

If a Company Commander is in doubt as to what punishment he should award for any particular offence, he should remand the accused and refer to Group Headquarters.

*Attention is drawn to the following* :—

K.R. 495 states that as forfeiture of pay for every day of absence is automatic under the Pay Warrant, the C.O. merely lets the soldier know the number of days for which pay is forfeited. This also applies to a Warrant Officer, although the C.O. has no power to give him any punishment. (*See also* A.A. 46 (8).)

The method of ascertaining what is a day's absence is laid down in Sec. 140, Army Act, as amended by the Army Annual Act, 1918.

K.R. 502 states that " absence without leave " terminates when a man is taken into custody (either military or civil).

R.P. 6 (*b*) prevents a C.O. increasing a sentence which has already been awarded (the award is complete when a man has left the presence of the officer making the award).

### 4. *Court-Martial Procedure.*

If the O.C. Company considers that the offence is one for which he cannot award a sufficient punishment he will refer it to the O.C. Group Headquarters. The latter will either deal with the case himself or direct that a court martial shall be applied for.

The G.O.C. Corps, or Base or Administrative Area Commandant, is the " Superior Authority," para. 548 K.R. (*See* G.R.O. 2472.)

K.R. 496 states that where a man elects trial he should usually be allowed to reconsider his decision on the following day.

K.R. 490 A. states that a man electing trial may, pending such trial, be released by the C.O. if circumstances warrant. O.C., Group Headquarters, should be consulted before this is done.

On application for court martial the following papers must be forwarded :—

- (i) Application for a court martial (A.F. B.116), with Medical Certificate completed. (A.F. B.241.)
- (ii) Charge sheet—(A.F. B. 2069)—which must be signed by O.C. Company.
- (iii) Certified true copy of Conduct Sheet. (A.F. B.122.)
- (iv) Summary of evidence.

(v) Any exhibits or documents relating to the case.

(vi) List of witnesses for the prosecution and defence. (With their present stations.)

(vii) Statement as to character and particulars of service of the accused. (A.F. B.296.)

## 5. *Charge Sheet.*

If the C.O. has any doubt as to the proper form of charge, he should make a short epitome of the statements of each witness who has been before him when investigating the case, so that he can see what they have actually stated. He should then compare this with the Forms of Charges in Appendix I of the Rules of Procedure (Manual of Military Law), until he comes to a heading, or headings, which he thinks will suit the case. He will then note the section under which the particular offence comes, and should then turn to the " Further Illustrations of Charges " in the same appendix, and see what forms are given by referring to the section, or sections, in the margin, under which he has found the charges.

If in doubt, section 40 will be found to cover practically any offence. (*See* " Further Illustrations of Charges," Nos. 72 to 77.)

A specimen form of Charge Sheet is shown on page 659, Manual of Military Law. If a soldier elects to be tried by court martial, the words " Elects Trial " should be written prominently on A.F. A.3 and on the charge sheet.

Whenever a Private or N.C.O. is committed for trial by court martial his permanent rank and any acting rank or lance rank or appointment held by him should invariably be shown, *e.g.,*

> Private (Acting Corporal) A.B., or
> Private (Acting Sergeant) C.D., or
> Corporal (Acting Company-Sergeant-Major) E.F.

## 6. *Summary of Evidence.*

(*See* Rule of Procedure 4, (*c*), (*d*), (*e*) and form in which it should be taken in S.S. 412, a Circular Memorandum on Courts Martial.

In taking a summary of evidence the following procedure should be adopted :—

(i) The accused, under escort, and all witnesses for prosecution or defence should be paraded.

(ii) The taking of the Summary should then be commenced. Only one witness at a time should be present, the remainder being ordered to stand by.

(iii) It must be in the handwriting of the O.C. Company, or an officer deputed by him.

(iv) It must be written on foolscap (if obtainable).

(v) The accused must be present.

(vi) Only the exact words used by the witnesses should be written down, and the summary should be free from any expression of opinion, or conjecture. All hearsay and other inadmissible evidence must be excluded.

(vii) On a charge of drunkenness a witness must definitely say that a man is " drunk " or " sober " and must be prepared to give reasons for his opinion, if necessary. In law there is no intermediate state.

(viii) The statement of each witness should be read over to him and signed by him in the presence of the accused. If he is unable to write he should make his mark in the presence of a witness, who must affix his signature thereto.

(ix) The accused can ask any questions relevant to his case. After a witness has completed and signed his statement, the questions with the answers should be added in writing to the evidence taken down.

(x) The accused can demand that the witnesses shall be put on oath.

(xi) The accused must be warned that he need not make any statement unless he wishes to do so, and that any statement made may be used against him.

(xii) Any statement made by the accused material to his defence shall be added in writing and signed by him.

(xiii) Witnesses for the defence will not have a summary of their evidence taken, unless the accused requests that this should be done, or they have already made statements.

(xiv) The officer taking the summary must be careful to complete it as shown in the Circular Memorandum referred to.

(xv) When a witness produces a document the officer taking the summary will note this in the text of the evidence, as follows :—" I produce a certified extract from the Order book of the 100th Labour Company." (Document put in marked " Exhibit ' A.' ".)

(xvi) Any exhibits (documents or otherwise) will be marked by the officer taking the summary, as follows :—

> " This is the exhibit marked ' A ' referred to in the evidence of——————————————— "

This should be signed by the officer taking the summary.

(xvii) When the papers mentioned in para. 13 are completed, they are forwarded to O.C., Group Headquarters, by whom they are forwarded to the Formation, or Base, or Area Commandant (on the L. of C.) the " Superior Authority," for deciding whether a court-martial should be convened.

(xviii) The matter is now out of the hands of the O.C. Company, who will receive all further instructions through the Group Headquarters. Full notes on court-martial procedure are contained in the Circular Memorandum referred to.

### 7. *Promulgation.*

(i) The finding and sentence passed by a court martial are " promulgated " after confirmation by superior authority.

(ii) This is done, whenever practicable, by being read out on parade, or in such other manner as may be directed for the particular occasion, but notice to the offender of the charge, finding, sentence and confirmation will be sufficient promulgation. In all cases however, the promulgation must include the communication of the foregoing particulars to the accused. (*See* Note to Sec. 53 Army Act, page 604 Manual of Military Law, and King's Regulations 593).

(iii) The officer who has promulgated the sentence should insert a minute at the foot of page 3 of A.F. A.3, to read as follows :—
Promulgated and extracts taken at
this          day of          19  .

### 8. *Rules for Field Punishment No. 1.*

If possible, F.P. should not be carried out in the Unit.

Group Commanders should always try to make arrangements with the nearest A.P.M. for the punishment to be carried out centrally. But if F.P. has to be carried out regimentally the following rules should be observed.

(i) The prisoner should be tied to an object in view of his comrades (but not of civilians) for 2 hours for not more than 3 out of 4 consecutive days up to 21 days. As far as possible this will take place between 2 p.m. and 4 p.m.

(ii) The soldier must be attached to an object so as to be standing firmly on his feet, which if tied, must not be more than 12 inches apart, and it must be possible for him to move each foot at least 3 inches. If he is tied round the body there must be no restriction of his breathing. If his arms or wrists are tied, there must be 6 inches of play between them and the fixed object. His arms must hang either by the side of his body, or behind his back. Irons should be used when possible, but straps or ropes may be used in lieu of them when necessary. Any straps or ropes used for this purpose must be of sufficient width that they inflict no bodily harm and leave no permanent mark on the offender.

(iii) There should be total prohibition of smoking and rum rations, and the prisoner should be prohibited from entering an estaminet.

(iv) All possible fatigues.

(v) Deduction of pay for every day of F.P awarded by F.G.C.M. or C.O. is automatic.

(vi) The prisoner should be from 6 p.m. to 6 a.m. in a guard room. Prisoner only to be allowed his blankets and must sleep on the floor, if it is stone he may be allowed straw.

(vii) His place on the leave roster will be decided by the O.C. Group.

(viii) Pack drill for at least 1 hour.

(ix) Rations—tea, bully beef and biscuits, but this may be left to the judgment of the Group Commander, who will conform to the orders of the formation.

(x) No regimental additions, or amendments, are to be made to above as A.P.M.'s are responsible for uniformity, and visit units to see that the above are strictly carried out.

### 9. *Courts of Enquiry.*

(See K.R. para. 666 *et seq.* and G.R.O. 2884 and SS. 617 issued therewith.)

Proceedings of Courts of Enquiry will be forwarded through Group H.Q. to D.A.G. Base, Q.M.G., or President, Claims Commission, as the case may be. Proceedings must be completed in every respect before despatch.

Special attention is drawn to directions given in para. 674 (iv) K.R. Proceedings of Courts of Enquiry under K.R. 674 will be forwarded by Group H.Q. for confirmation by G.O.C. Formation, or by Base, or Administrative Area, Commandant in L. of C. Area.

---

## CHAPTER IX.—SUPPLIES, ORDNANCE STORES AND STATIONERY.

1. Units will indent for Supplies and Ordnance Stores as directed by the Group Commander, either through Group Headquarters or direct on the A.S.C. or A.O.D.

In the latter case the Group Commander will see that the Company Commander is informed as to whom indents should be rendered.

In Army Areas supplies are issued by :—

    1. Railhead Supply Officers.

    2. S.O. Army or Corps Troops M.T. Company.

    3. S.S.O. Divisional train through S.O. Brigade.

To any one of whom indents may be rendered according to the proximity of the company to a railhead or refilling point.

Ordnance Stores are obtained through the O.O. Army Troops or O.O. Corps Troops as the case may be.

On the L. of C. indents for Supplies are submitted to the O.C. Detail Issue Store, and indents for Ordnance Stores to the Ordnance Officer of the place, or area, in which the unit is quartered.

## 2. *Notes on Indenting.*

Rations, Forage, Fuel and Light. (*See* G.R.O. 2523 and S.S. 571). The indent (A.B. 55) is made out in triplicate, two copies being handed to Supply Officer, and one copy retained for reference. The weighing of all supplies at refilling points, and detail issue stores, should be carefully checked.

Clothing Stores and Equipment. (*See* G.R.O. 1193 and S.S. 340). The Indent Form A.F. G. 994 is used, two copies being sent to the Ordnance Officer and one retained for reference. The equipment and clothing are issued by A.O.D. as authorised in Mobilization Store Tables and G.R.Os. Copies of Mobilization Store Tables can be obtained from Publications, Boulogne.

The issue of tailors' tools is governed by G.R.Os. 2168 and 2326.

When indenting for clothing, stores and equipment, the authority for the issue should, whenever possible, be quoted on the indent submitted to Ordnance.

A great deal of useful information as to the method of obtaining stores and supplies can be obtained from the Field Service Pocket Book.

When indenting for clothing, &c., to replace worn out or damaged clothing, a certificate to the effect that the articles required are to replace unserviceable or worn-out clothing must be given signed by the officer signing the indent.

## 3. *Unserviceable Stores.*

All the authorised equipment and stores on charge of a unit will be checked periodically. All articles lost or rendered unserviceable through neglect will be charged for.

A Board should sit on all clothing to be condemned as unserviceable. It should consist of two officers, one of whom should be the Group Quartermaster if available.

All worn-out and unserviceable equipment must be returned to Ordnance, for disposal. The unserviceable clothing will be returned to the Base as rags under existing orders for the disposal of unserviceable clothing.

A record will be kept of issues to individuals of personal equipment clothing and necessaries. Replacement will only be made on production of the old articles. A man will be charged for losses of equipment, clothing and necessaries, if lost or becoming unserviceable through negligence.

In the case of clothing or equipment being rendered unserviceable, due to neglect on the part of any man, the man concerned will be charged with the cost of the article, as priced on A.F. W. 3315. (*See* G.R.Os. 1228, 1719, and 420 as amended by 1865, in Part II. Extracts from G.R.Os. S.S. 340, also G.R.Os. 3859 and 3900.)

The amount in question must be entered as a debit in the man's Pay Book, A.B. 64, and particulars entered on the proper A.F. W. 3069, in duplicate, signed by the man accepting the debit; when completed and signed by the O.C. this form is forwarded to the Command Paymaster i/c Clearing House, Base, for the Regimental Paymaster's requirements.

Officers' clothing, equipment and necessaries may be obtained from the A.O.D. on payment. The procedure to be adopted when demanding or purchasing direct is laid down in G.R.Os. 2761, 2876, 3040, and 3841.

**Stationery and Publications** are supplied by the Army Printing and Stationery Service (*see* Extracts from G.R.Os. Part I, especially G.R.O. 2398.)

---

## CHAPTER X.—ECONOMY AND SALVAGE.

1. Economy in Food.—Economy in the use of food, stores and equipment is of the first importance.

The full ration as laid down in G.R.Os., if properly used, is more than sufficient for units of the strength of Labour Companies, and economy should be effected by means of "underdrawals," *i.e.*, components of the ration not required should not be indented for.

Os.C. units should pay special attention to the information given in S.S. 615 "Cooking in the Field," which can be obtained from Publications, Boulogne.

With the aid of this book there can be no excuse for waste or misuse of rations.

There are instructors in catering in the Army Areas and in the L. of C. Area, and their advice and assistance should always be sought. There are schools of cookery to which suitable men should be sent for instruction.

2. Economy in Fuel.—All available firewood should be collected and stored for winter consumption. Much can be done in the way of salvage.

Coal dust should be mixed with a proportion of clay and made into balls. This is practicable in rear areas, and utilizes the full fuel properties of coal dust, a large proportion of which would otherwise be waste.

Brick fireplaces suitable for wood burning in offices and other permanent quarters should be made.

3. **Economy in Office Stationery.**—Every effort must be made to economise in paper and in office stationery of all kinds. (*See* G.R.O. 2848.)

4. **Economy in Stores and Equipment.**—Stores, even when damaged or apparently valueless, are not to be thrown away or abandoned. Tools, equipment, wheels, wire—anything and everything that is of use to an army—must be saved, as it can be turned to account by the Army Ordnance Department.

Os.C. Companies should make careful note of the orders and instructions issued from time to time for the disposal of worn articles of clothing and equipment, &c.

Attention is drawn to G.R.O. 420 (in extracts Part II) and F.S.R., Part II, Sect. 76.

5. Units at work on roads and in areas recently occupied by troops will render great service by collecting salvage such as petrol tins, rubber, old tyres, steel helmets, gas helmets, &c., and form a dump at Company H.Q.

Group H.Q. should be notified of the quantity of materials salved, location of dump, and the transport needed to collect. The Group H.Q. will arrange with the Labour Commandant or Salvage Officer for the material to be removed.

----

## CHAPTER XI.—ACCOMMODATION.

Procedure for obtaining billets is fully explained in A.B. 397 and S.S. 396, " Instructions as to Requisitions, Billeting and Quartering in France and Belgium." An advanced party should always be sent to take over and prepare billets, and a party left to clean up.

In order to improve billets it has been necessary for units to provide articles, both for the convenience of the troops and for sanitary purposes, *e.g.*, wash-tubs, baths, ablution benches, watering troughs, pumps, stoves, &c. The removal of such articles by troops when they vacate billets, which are to be occupied by relieving troops, causes not only great waste of money (because the articles have to be replaced) but also much ill-feeling, and the practice must be discontinued. All such articles are *Billet Equipment.* They will be treated in the same way as barrack equipment in peace, and must be handed over regularly to incoming by outgoing units. To enable this to be done properly, and to avoid the risk of removal of articles by inhabitants and others, the billet-wardens of the outgoing troops will be left in the billets whenever possible, until the incoming troops, or their billet wardens, have actually entered the billets. Outgoing units will obtain from incoming units *certificates* to the effect that the billets have been taken over in a satisfactory condition, and that the billet equipment agrees with the inventory.

Rules to be observed on the evacuation of quarters, billets, camps or bivouacs :—

(i) Huts, shelters and straw will not be burnt.

(ii) Rubbish will be burnt.

(iii) All waste papers, documents, &c., will be burnt.

(iv) Signboards, or any other indications which would give information regarding the troops which have occupied the ground, will be removed.

(v) Sites of latrines will be marked by a large letter " L " formed of stones, or by a notice board.

In order to cause as little inconvenience as possible to the inhabitants, latrines, if dug in gardens, &c., will be grouped.

If all ranks and units adopt the rule of leaving billets even a little cleaner and more comfortable than they found them, a marked improvement would soon take place. The removal of property, fixtures and equipment from billets is strictly forbidden ; it can only result in lowering the general standard of comfort of troops.

The same remarks apply to Standing Camps with either hutting or tentage accommodation.

---

## CHAPTER XII.—HORSE MANAGEMENT.

In order to maintain the efficiency of Transport, drivers must be taught to consider the comfort and condition of their horses before their own. To ensure this, it is absolutely necessary that officers should take a personal interest in the horses, and the turnout of the harness and wagons.

1. Feeding.—" Little and often " is the principle on which feeding should be carried out. Heavy draught horses should be fed four times a day ; the last feed at night should consist mainly of hay.

Feeding off the ground should not be allowed—it encourages dirty feeding in the horse, and tends to sand colic and other diseases.

No horse or mule should be allowed to go out on duty without a feed in the nosebag.

Every advantage should be taken of grazing, when grass is available, and during the winter much advantage can be gained by the use of carrots, turnips, mangolds, and a small amount of linseed cake, when it can be got.

Rock salt is very useful, and a small piece should be kept in every manger, where horses are accommodated in stables.

Nosebags must be kept clean, turned inside out after the horse has finished his feed, and thoroughly scrubbed once a week.

For the scale of rations and equivalents, see S.S.571. Officers Commanding should study the scale laid down, and obtain suitable equivalents, whenever possible, in order to make a variation in the feeding.

2. Watering.—Horses should be watered before feeding; *never* immediately afterwards.

When on the march, every opportunity of clean water should be taken for giving the horse a drink, but on no account should horses be walked into muddy or stagnant water. Bits should be removed before the horses are watered, but horses should be bitted when marched to water.

All buckets and drinking utensils must be kept scrupulously clean, and if a horse shows any sign of cold—running at the nose or sore throat—a separate bucket should be set aside for him.

3. Grooming.—Grooming is necessary for horses in work. It must be thorough and systematic.

Special attention should be given to head, ears, mane, tail, dock, and feet.

Legs should not be washed, but should be dry groomed.

The feet should be carefully picked out first thing in the morning, and on harnessing up and returning from work. Each driver should be in possession of a hoof-pick, which can be made out of an old horseshoe. On no account should drivers be allowed to use jack-knives, or marlin spikes, for this purpose.

Officers Commanding should ensure that each driver is in possession of a grooming kit for each horse; nothing spreads disease more quickly than using the same grooming kit for several horses.

Horses should be inspected daily by an officer.

4. Shoeing.—Special attention should be paid to the condition of shoes. As a general rule, horses require shoeing once in every three weeks to a month.

5. Harness and Saddlery.—Fitting: a frequent cause of horses becoming inefficient is the ill-fitting of harness and saddlery. Three frequent faults are :—

   (*a*) Breast collar too low.
   (*b*) Breeching too loose and too long.
   (*c*) Loin strap too short.

Harness must be kept clean, soft and pliable.

Harness and saddlery should be cleaned every day, immediately the grooming of the horse has been finished; and once a week the whole set should be stripped, *i.e.*, every buckle undone and strap separated, and thoroughly scrubbed with disinfectant.

As soon as a gall is noticed, its cause must be inquired into and remedied. It is not sufficient merely to treat the gall. In any case in which it is apparent that the gall is due to neglect, or careless fitting of harness, disciplinary action should be taken against the driver.

**6. Clothing.**—During the summer and warm weather, horses are better without rugs, but during the winter, one rug at least per animal is necessary for those picketed in the open.

A rug, even if wet through, is an advantage, but if a horse comes in soaked, it is advisable, after rubbing him well down with straw or hay, to put a little straw or hay under the rug along the back.

Rugs should be marked with the number of the horse, to ensure the same one being constantly used for the same animal.

**7. Picket Lines.**—The best form of picket line is breast-high.

Standings must be kept clean, and holes filled up; few things are more detrimental to horses than standing in water or liquid mud.

**8. Skin Diseases.**—Veterinary advice should be sought on the first appearance of any disease or irritation of the skin or discharge from the eyes or nostrils. No animal should be placed in a stable until the building has been passed by a Veterinary Officer or the Town Major in whose area it is located. Neglect of these precautions is often the means of spreading infectious diseases such as mange.

---

### CHAPTER XIII.—GENERAL.

1. Although Labour units may not be employed in active military operations, they are constantly in touch with fighting troops. They must avoid talking about any movements of troops, or military operations. Such apparently trivial information as the position of a unit, or even of a man belonging to a special unit, may be most useful to the enemy, and it is impossible to know when or how such information may reach the enemy. The only safe course is not to mention anything of this nature in conversation, especially in public.

2. It cannot be too strongly impressed upon all ranks that they should not disclose information of a military nature, either in correspondence, while on leave in England, or in any other way.

**3** It is important that officers should be thoroughly acquainted with Censorship Orders for Troops in the Field. (Extracts from G.R.Os., Part 1.)

**4.** Attention is drawn to G.R.Os. 1709, **3065,** copies of which can be obtained from Publications Department on indent.

In every Labour Company a book is to be kept in which these orders will be pasted, and a nominal roll of officers will be entered in the book. All officers are to initial this book as an acknowledgment that they have read these orders, and each new officer joining will sign the book on the day he joins. Os.C. Groups will inspect the books from time to time.

G.R.O.1709 should be read on parade at least once every month.

**5.** It should be impressed upon all ranks that in describing their experiences in letters no good is obtained, but actual harm may be done, by exaggerating the experiences of the writer. It not only causes mental anxiety to relatives and friends, but tends to spread alarm and despondency at home, the only result being to help the enemy.

### 6. *Our Allies.*

Our Allies are just as anxious for victory as we are. The French and the Belgians have suffered more than we have, but, in spite of it, never complain. Hence they should receive every consideration at our hands. As we are in their countries we should respect their customs and wishes as much as we can. In all our relations with any of our Allies, it is obviously desirable for us to be polite and courteous in our dealings with them. It must be borne in mind that every misunderstanding or unpleasantness tends to weaken our alliance and to help the enemy.

All ranks will be most particular in saluting the officers of our Allies.

### 7 *Postal Service.*

(*See* Extracts G.R.Os., Part II.)—With each Supply Column there are two Postal Lorries, and a Postal Staff of a corporal and two men, who convey Mails to re-filling points. Here the N.C.O. from each Field Post Office supervises the distribution of the mails to the postal orderlies of the Group, who attend with their regimental transport to receive mails. The post orderlies take mails to their units, and distribute them regimentally. At all points of transfer, receipts will be given for the number of bags received.

Postal orderlies should be in possession of A.B. 426 and obtain a signature for all registered packets.

Letters for posting are delivered to Field Post Offices.

The correct addresses of units of the Labour Corps are :—

(a)     No.     Rank,     Name,
               H.Q. No.     Labour Group,
or                         B.E.F., France.

(b)     No.     Labour Company,
                         B.E.F., France.

---

## CHAPTER XIV.—TRANSPORT.

The decision as to whether a Labour Company shall have its own transport or not rests with the G.O.C. the Formation under which it is working. The need for economy in transport is urgent. It is, for example, possible that in some Groups the location and work of two Labour units may be such that the transport establishment of one company will suffice for two.

The following establishment shows the *maximum* quantity of transport authorised for a Labour Company : this should not be indented for if less will suffice. G.O.C. Formation will decide if this transport is necessary.

| Detail. | Vehicles. | Drivers, A.S.C. | Horses. | |
|---|---|---|---|---|
| | | | Draught. | Heavy Draught. |
| *First Line.* | | | | |
| Carts, officers' mess ... ... | 1 | 1 | 1 | ... |
| Carts (Maltese, for medical equipment) ... ... ... ... | 1 | (*g*) | 1 | ... |
| Carts, water ... ... ... | 1 | 1 | 2 | ... |
| Wagons, G.S., or carts, tip, for tools ... ... ... ... | 2 | 2 | ... | 4 |
| Driver for spare draught horse ... | ... | 1 | 1 | ... |
| Driver, spare ... ... ... | ... | 1 | ... | ... |
| *Second Line.* | | | | |
| Wagons, G.S., for baggage and supplies ... ... ... ... | 2 | 2 | ... | 4 |
| TOTAL ... | 7 | 8 | 5 | 8 |

(*g*) Driven by M.O.'s private.

### CHAPTER XV.—EMPLOYMENT COMPANIES.

1. Employment Companies are divided as follows :—

   (a) Divisional Companies.
   (b) Area Employment Companies.

Included in Area Employment Companies, under (b), are :—

   (i) Army Headquarters (Area) Employment Companies.
   (ii) Corps (Area) Employment Companies.

G.O.C., L. of C., has at his disposal a number of Area Employment Companies, and Garrison Guard Companies, as a pool to meet emergencies.

These units, when not otherwise required, are used in the Labour Pool.

The underlying principle in the formation of all these units is to control what were formerly known as " P.B. men," and also extra regimental employment.

Before the formation of these units, and their inclusion in the Labour Corps, " P.B." men were allotted to Armies, and by them to corps, &c. In addition to these men, a large number of men were extra regimentally employed. To such an extent had this grown, that it became difficult to check the fighting strength of units.

All Divisional and Army and Corps Headquarters (Area) Employment Companies will be specially allotted to the Headquarters concerned for the distribution and employment of personnel, and will not be included in Labour Groups. These companies will move with the Formations to which they are attached. Area Employment Companies remain in the area to which they are allotted, and will be posted to an existing Labour Group.

All questions affecting postings, promotions, &c., of officers in Divisional and Army and Corps (Area) Employment Companies, will be referred to the Labour Commandant concerned. Area Employment Companies will be dealt with in the same way as Labour Companies, by the Labour Commandant concerned, both as regards their personnel and also their allotment and employment.

Cross postings of personnel according to medical categories between Labour and Area Employment Companies and *vice versa*, will be carried out by Labour Commandants in Army Areas, or through Base or Area Headquarters in the L. of C. Area.

In making out A.F. B. 213 Os.C. Companies should state in detail what classes of men are required, *e.g.*, cooks, orderlies, &c.

Forty Category " A " men are allowed in the establishment of a Divisional Employment Company, but should be withdrawn whenever it is possible to replace them by " B " men.

Only Category " B " men are allowed in Area Employment Companies.

## 2. *War Establishments.*

The War Establishment of—(1) a Divisional Employment Company Labour Corps, and (2) an Area Employment Company, Labour Corps (provided by A.C.I. **837** of July 23, 1917), is :—

| Detail. | Headquarters. | For employments. | Total. |
|---|---|---|---|
| Major or captain...　...　... | 1 | ... | 1 |
| Subaltern　...　...　... | 1 | ... | 1 |
| Total officers　...　... | 2 | ... | 2 |
| Company quartermaster serjeant (a)　...　...　... | 1 | ... | 1 |
| Orderly-room clerk　...　... | 1 | ... | 1 |
| N.C.Os. and privates (b)　... | ... | 270 | 270 |
| Batman ...　...　...　... | 1 | ... | 1 |
| Total company　...　... | 5 | 270 | 275 |

(*a*) To perform the duties of company serjeant-major and company quartermaster-serjeant.

(*b*) Serjeants, corporals, and lance-corporals for purposes of administration and discipline will only be appointed as the Commander-in-Chief may direct, and in no case will the number exceed the following proportion:—

> 1 serjeant for each 60 privates.
> 1 corporal for each 30 privates.
> 1 lance-corporal for each 24 privates.

The above numbers coming out of the establishment of the company.

## 3. *Transport.*

No scale has been laid down, and arrangements for transport when required must be made with the Formation to which the Company is attached, or the Area Commandant in whose area a Company is stationed.

A horse, or bicycle, for the O.C. Company can be drawn if sanctioned by the G.O.C.

## 4. *Clothing.*

Same scale as for infantry (*see* Extracts, G.R.Os., Part II.)

## 5. *Equipment.*

To be on the same scale as infantry, less arms and ammunition.

Arms and ammunition are issued on the scale of 25 per cent. of the unit.

Mobilisation Store Table A.F. G. 1098-371.

## 6. *Duties.*

The personnel of a Divisional Employment Company provides the following duties :—

| | |
|---|---:|
| Canteens ... ... ... ... ... | 10 |
| Cooks, D.H.Q. ... ... ... ... ... | 6 |
| ,, Brigade Headquarters ... ... | 9 |
| Band ... ... ... ... ... ... | 30 |
| Train loaders ... ... ... ... ... | 75 |
| Clerks, D.H.Q. ... ... ... ... ... | 8 |
| ,, Brigade Headquarters ... ... | 6 |
| ,, R.A. Headquarters ... ... ... | 2 |
| Orderlies, D.H.Q. ... ... ... ... | 16 |
| Entertainments... ... ... ... ... | 12 |
| Salvage ... ... ... ... ... ... | 50 |
| Sanitary ... ... ... ... ... | 16 |
| General duties ... ... ... ... ... | 17 |
| Shoemakers' shop ... ... . ... ... | 5 |
| Baths ... ... ... ... ... ... | 8 |
| | 270 |

The personnel of an Army Headquarters (Area) Employment Company provides the following duties :—

| | |
|---|---:|
| Canteens ... ... ... ... ... | 4 |
| Cooks ... ... ... ... ... ... | 28 |
| Clerks ... ... ... ... ... ... | 30 |
| Orderlies ... ... ... ... ... | 70 |
| Guards ... ... ... ... ... ... | 36 |
| General duties ... ... ... ... ... | 90 |
| Sanitary ... ... ... ... ... | 12 |
| | 270 |

The establishment of a Corps Headquarters (Area) Employment Company is slightly reduced, and consists of :—

| | |
|---|---:|
| Captain or subaltern ... ... ... ... | 1 |
| C.Q.M.S.... ... ... ... ... ... | 1 |
| Orderly-room clerk ... ... ... ... | 1 |
| Batman ... ... ... ... ... ... | 1 |
| Employments ... ... ... ... ... | 116 |
| | 120 |

It finds the following duties :—

| | |
|---|---:|
| Canteens ... ... ... ... ... | 4 |
| Cooks ... ... ... ... ... ... | 11 |
| Clerks ... ... ... ... ... ... | 14 |
| Orderlies ... ... ... ... ... | 24 |
| Police ... ... ... ... ... ... | 8 |
| Butchers, tailors, shoemakers... ... ... | 8 |
| General duties ... ... ... ... ... | 35 |
| Sanitary ... ... ... ... ... | 12 |
| | 116 |

## CHAPTER XVI.—THE MIDDLESEX REGIMENT (ALIENS).

1. There are seven of these companies, numbered 1st, 2nd, 3rd, 4th, 5th, 6th and 7th Infantry Labour Companies of the Middlesex Regiment.

The War Establishment and Scale of Clothing and Equipment of these companies are the same as for British Labour Companies.

These units consist of men who are naturalised British subjects of enemy alien parentage.

### 2. *Where and How they can be employed.*

These companies must only be employed North of a line Abbeville—Amiens, but not *at* or *near* a Base Port, nor in the area of the Seine-Inferieure.

They must not be employed within 16 kilometres of the front line, nor on Ammunition work, nor in the immediate vicinity of P. of W. Companies. It is preferable to employ them in sparsely populated places.

It is considered dangerous from the point of view of counter-espionage that individual men from Alien Labour Companies should be detached for employment in which they may be in a position to obtain information, and are perhaps not under strict supervision.

They must therefore, never be employed as mess cooks, waiters, barbers, clerks or orderlies, or in officers' clubs or Cinemas, or in any position in which they could obtain information useful to the enemy.

### 3. *Movements and Leave.*

The movements of these units are to be notified to the Intelligence Branch of the General Staff.

Notification that leave has been granted to the personnel of Alien Labour Companies should be forwarded to A.G., G.H.Q., accompanied by a statement, at least one week before any alien proceeds on leave, showing

    (i) Period of leave and dates.

    (ii) Destination and address.

    (iii) Date of last leave. (For further instructions with regard to personnel of Alien Labour Companies proceeding on leave, *see* G.R.O. 4210).

The circulation of these units should be restricted as much as possible. No men should be permitted to leave the vicinity of their company without being provided with a regulation pass duly signed and stamped.

*Reinforcements and Casualties.*

The Base Depot of these companies is " J " Base Depot at Etaples and *not* the Labour Corps Base Depot at Boulogne.

All men, casuals, reinforcements or otherwise, will be sent there. No men whether " A " or " B " categories will be retained at the Base, but will be returned to their own units as soon as possible.

Any men unfit for service in France will be returned to the 30th and 31st Works Battalions, Middlesex Regiment, according to whichever of them they originally belonged. No men of these companies will be transferred or posted to any other unit, or branch of the Service, without special War Office authority.

## CHAPTER XVII.—OTHER LABOUR COMPANIES.

There are Canadian Labour units. They come under the Controller of Labour for allotment, but are not under a Group Headquarters. They are permanently allotted for work in the Canadian Corps Area.

There are Russian Companies formed of men of Russian parentage naturalised in England. Their Establishment is the same as for a British Labour Company. There is no restriction on their employment.

There are seven companies in France of the Non-Combatant Corps.

Establishment :—

| Detail. | | Officers. | Staff-serjeants and serjeants. | Rank and file. | Total. | Remarks. |
|---|---|---|---|---|---|---|
| Captain (or subaltern) | ... | 1 | ... | ... | 1 | (a) To perform the duties of both C.S.M. and C.Q.M.S. |
| Colour-serjeant (a) ... | ... | ... | 1 | ... | 1 | |
| Serjeants ... ... | ... | ... | 1 | ... | 1 | |
| Corporals ... ... | ... | ... | ... | 2 | 2 | |
| Lance-corporals ... | ... | ... | ... | 4 | 4 | |
| Privates ... ... | ... | ... | ... | 94 | 94 | |
| Total ... ... | ... | 1 | 2 | 100 | 103 | |

There will not be any reinforcements sent out for these companies.

They may be employed in Road making, Hutting, Timber cutting, Quarrying, Sanitary work, Loading and unloading of ships and vehicles, and Digging, provided they are not employed in the firing line.

They should not be armed or trained with arms of any description. On the whole they are good workers, and the majority are educated.

It is not desirable that men of the N.C.C. should be given work which is lighter than, or more congenial than, that given to men of British Labour Companies in the same locality. It should be remembered that the majority of these men are really "A" men, and are quite capable of doing considerably harder work than men of lower categories.

Coloured Labour units are dealt with in special chapters, but some matters affecting them generally may be noted here.

The Coloured Labour Units, being engaged on special terms, are not to be located in forward areas where camps or work are liable to hostile shelling. As a rule, therefore, the Coloured Labour Units will be kept outside about a 16 kilometre zone from the front line.

Owing to the special conditions which apply to the accommodation required by S.A.N.L. Cos. and C.L. Cos. it is necessary that Commandants concerned should notify direct, Adviser S.A.N.L.C., or Adviser, C.L.C., when a compound for reception of natives or Chinese has been prepared, in order that the officer concerned may inspect it before occupation.

As regards inoculation the D.G.M.S. has agreed to the following procedure :—

    (i) Natives to be inoculated at the stations to which they are sent for work on arrival in this country, under arrangements to be made by the Medical Authorities concerned.

    (ii) The number of men inoculated on one day at any place not to exceed 50, and only one batch of 50 at a time to be incapacitated for work.

Full information as regards Prisoner of War Companies is contained in S.S. 457.

## CHAPTER XVIII.—INDIAN LABOUR.

1. The War Establishment of a Company Indian Labour Corps is :—

| Details. | British. | | Indians. | | | Riding Horses. | Bicycles. |
|---|---|---|---|---|---|---|---|
| | Officers. | Staff Serjeants. | N.C.O.'s. | Rank and File. | Total. | | |
| Major or Captain ... ... | 1 | | | | 1 | (a) | (a 2 |
| Subalterns ... ... ... | 4 | | | | 4 | | |
| Havildar Major ... ... | | | 1 | | 1 | | |
| Pay Havildar ... ... | | | 1 | | 1 | | |
| Havildars ... ... ... | | | 8 | | 8 | | |
| Naiks ... ... ... | | | 21(b) | | 21 | | |
| Labourers ... ... ... | | | | 451(c) | 451 | | |
| Batmen ... ... ... | | | | 5 | 5 | | |
| Sweepers ... ... ... | | | | 4 | 4 | | |
| Bhisties ... ... ... | | | | 4 | 4 | | |
| Total (excluding attached ... ... | 5 | | 31 | 464 | 500 | | 2 |
| *Attached(d).* | | | | | | | |
| Foremen ... ... ... | | 4 | | | 4 | | |
| Total (including attached) ... | 5 | 4 | 31 | 464 | 504 | | 2 |

A Company consists of a Headquarters and 4 Platoons. Each Platoon consists of 2 Sections each under a Havildar. Each Section consists of 2 Sub-sections each under a Naik.

Transport as for a British Labour Company.

(a) One riding horse or bicycle for the O.C. Company is allowed in cases where the G.O.C. Formation considers such an issue is necessary.

(b) Includes 1 Cook and 2 Clerks for Orderly Room and 2 Interpreters.

(c) Includes Artificers.

(d) When specially authorised.

### 2. *Terms of Engagement.*

The men are enrolled under the Indian Army Act for general service, and for " one year or for the period of the war," whichever is the less.

### 3. *Base Depot and Records.*

The Base Depot is at MARSEILLES, and will accommodate 500 O.R. Provision for an extension with tented accommodation up to 4,000 has been made.

*Records* are kept by the Indian Section, G.H.Q., 3rd Echelon.

### 4. *Casualty Returns.*

These are rendered on Sundays on A.F. B. 213M (*see* Extracts from G.R.Os., Part I, and Field Service Regulations, Part II, Section 132). A.F. B. 213 can be used for Native personnel if A.F. B. 213M cannot be obtained.

A detail of the figures shown against the first item on the front of the form, *i.e.*, " Effective strength of unit," should be given in the " Remarks " column. This should show numbers *by ranks* separately for—(*a*) British Officers ; (*b*) Indian Officers ; (*c*) British other ranks ; (*d*) Indian other ranks ; and (*e*) Followers (*e.g.*, labourers, sweepers and Bhisties).

A separate return showing deficiencies by ranks, as in para. 2, will also be furnished.

The following should be noted in regard to the detail called for on the reverse of the form.

It is most important in order that individuals' records of field service may be correctly compiled that the following be very carefully entered :—

- (i) All casualties in the field, *i.e.*, deaths, wounds (accidental or otherwise, and whether necessitating admission to Hospital or not) and admissions to and discharges from Hospital.

- (ii) All punishments awarded supported by A.F. B. 2069.

- (iii) Promotions and appointments :—In the case of officers drawing staff pay, forenoon or afternoon should be given with the date on which they took over or relinquished their appointment.

- (iv) Transfers showing whether permanent, or temporary, including all leave granted.

- (v) All dates given for purposes of record should be the actual date, and the reference on the reverse of the form to the ration return should be ignored.

### 5. *Pay and Accounting.*

Indian labour was originally organised in India on a Corps basis and was despatched as " Corps " about 2,000 strong.

Each " Corps " had a Commandant, 2 Assistant Commandants, and 4 Supervisors—one for each section of 500.

On arrival in FRANCE, the Corps were re-organised on a Company basis.

Some of the later Companies were organised as such in India. The War Establishment on which they were formed differs from that shown in these Notes, but they are now brought on to the same basis. The rates of pay are contained in 3rd Echelon (Indian Section), Letter No. 1/2752/17, dated 17th May, 1918.

Every man has on him I.A.F. K. 1157 (Followers Service Book), or A.B. 64 (Pay Book).

Accounts are passed through the Field Controller of Military Accounts, I.E.F. " A," France, as regards the British personnel ; through the Field Disbursing Officer, I.E.F. " A,'' Poona, as regards the Indian Military personnel ; and through the Chief Auditor, Non-Military Pay and Pension Accounts, as regards the Indian personnel other than the Indian Military personnel.

NOTE.—The Field C.M.A., I.E.F. " A," France, deals with the accounts of the British personnel only. The accounts of the Indian personnel are dealt with as above stated.

## 6. *Imprest Accounts.*

Money is drawn by Company Commanders on an " Imprest Account " (A.F. N. 1531A), and money disbursed as pay is shown on Acquittance Rolls (A.F. N. 1513).

A pamphlet has been issued by the F.C.M.A. entitled " Instructions for the guidance of Officers who hold their imprests from the Field Controller of Military Accounts, I.E.F. ' A.' "

This explains how to open and the method of using Imprest Accounts and Acquittance Rolls, and should be in the possession of every Company Commander.

The following note should be read as supplemental to the above pamphlet :—

All money received during the month should be shown on the Credit side of the Imprest Account (A.F. N. 1531A), and all payments made during the month should be shown on the Debtor side, or, in other words, all the receipts and payments during a month should invariably be shown in the Imprest Account for that month.

## 7. *Issue of Pay.*

All advances to men should be 5 francs or in multiples of 5 francs.

Advances of pay to men during any month should not exceed the net monthly pay due, *i.e.*, his gross pay less any deductions on account of family allotments, &c. It may, however, be necessary to relax slightly this rule for the first two months, on account of the men having had large advances of pay in India. If an individual underdraws advances he may draw the amount that has thus accumulated which can be calculated from his Service Book (I.A.F. K. 1175) or Pay Book (A.B. 64).

The net amount of pay due to a man can be ascertained from his pay book, which should show his monthly pay, &c., and the recoveries, if any, to be made monthly. If these particulars have not been entered up in the pay book this should be done as soon possible.

Each payment of advance should be entered up in the pay book of the individual, and the entry signed by the Officer who makes the payment.

Payments in the Field should be restricted as much as possible, and, in the case of men returning to India, only sufficient money should be given them as will meet their requirements for the period of the voyage.

## 8. *Acquittance Rolls.*

Advances should be made on Acquittance Rolls (Army Form N. 1513)—*see* Section III in the pamphlet above referred to.

The Acquittance Rolls are checked by the Field C.M.A., France, and then forwarded to the Field Disbursing Officer, I.E.F. " A," Poona, as regards the Indian Military personnel, and to the Chief Auditor, Dadar, Bombay, as regards Indian personnel other than the Indian Military personnel.

A supply of Imprest Account forms (Army Form N. 1531a), and Acquittance Roll forms (Army Form N. 1513) should be obtained from the Army Printing and Stationery Depot, HAVRE. Followers' Service Books (I.A.F. K. 1157) are not obtainable in this country, but Pay Books (A.B. 64) can be used in lieu, and if men are in possession of neither of these books, supplies of the latter can be obtained from the above source, mention being made in the application that they are required for Indians.

Personal advances of pay to British Officers of Labour Corps should not be paid through Imprest Accounts, but they should draw such advances direct from Field Cashiers on receipts. All others should draw advances on Acquittance rolls.

## 9. *Accommodation.*

The same as for British Troops, except cooking arrangements and latrines, which will be on the scale for Indian Troops.

Every endeavour should be made to hut Indian Labour during the winter months.

Company Officers will often have to prepare their own camps, or improve existing camps for occupation by their Companies.

In the summer sanitary precautions, especially against the spread of disease by flies, are the most important. In the winter the chief considerations are the warming of the huts and arrangements for drying clothes. In the summer men may be accommodated in tents. Huts are always provided in the winter. The average number for a bell tent should be 10, and in Adrian huts 70.

The best form of sleeping place is a continuous plank platform about 18 inches from the ground, and with a slight slope towards the middle of the hut. It is best made in sections hinged at the wall end so that the ground underneath may be swept every day.

These platforms can be washed down with creosol and water periodically. Kitchens or cook-houses should be walled and roofed with corrugated iron and floors cemented. Fireplaces are easily made with two iron rails or similar material supported on bricks or petrol tins filled with earth. A covered annex with smooth plank table for cutting up meat, and fly-proofed meat safes should be provided. The latter are particularly important in summer. Cooking accommodation should have regard to number of gangs or sections, and also to different Castes and religions. Ablution places should be on cemented floors, and be provided with a grease trap discharging into a soak pit or connected to an existing drainage system.

Latrines should be prepared by digging trenches not less than 8 feet in depth (10 is better), of a breadth to take the squatting form of covers with self-closing flaps. One place to every 20 men should be provided. These shonld be surrounded by a fence or screen of any available material, and should be roofed over in winter. When necessary arrangements should be made for washing at latrines, e.g., a concrete floor with graded channel discharging into a soak-pit. (Latrines of this pattern must also be provided at "Dumps" and "Railheads," and other places where Indian Labour is employed constantly.)

Urinals should also be provided at convenient places in the camp. Night pails for the same purposes should be placed close to the doors of each hut.

Drying sheds should be constructed. If possible the fire used for the drying shed should also be utilised in heating water for warm baths in an adjoining room.

A steam chamber should be provided for the disinfection of clothing.

### 10. *Rations, Canteens, Clothing, Stationery.*

*Rations, Fuel and Light* : as laid down in G.R.O. 2523 and S.S. 571 for Indian personnel.

*Canteens and Recreation Huts.*—A hut should be reserved or a suitable building constructed to serve as Recreation Room and Canteen, especially during the winter months. Canteens should be established in all camps. The E.F.C. provides facilities for stocking and maintaining these by arrangement with Group Commander. The Y.M.C.A. also gives assistance in these matters.

*Scale of Clothing*, see G.R.O. 2799.—The scale of clothing is ample, and in all probability some of the articles will not be required during the summer months. Os.C. Companies should take every precaution that only those articles actually required are drawn.

*Repairs of boots and clothing, &c.*—It is necessary to keep a few men always repairing boots and clothing. If the Company does not possess a sufficient number of men of the required trades, endeavour should be made to have men trained either by tradesmen in the Company or in some other Company. In the latter case application should be made to Group Commander. One or two men in each Company should be trained also in rough carpentering, if the Company does not possess carpenters. Certain tools may be drawn from Ordnance by Companies possessing carpenters (G.R.O. 2719, dated 19.10.17). In some Groups training schools for certain trades have been established in P. of W. Companies.

*Scale of Ordnance Stores, see* Mobilization Store Table, A.F. G. 1098/388, dated January, 1918.

*Army Forms, Books, and Stationery.*—Indents should be sent to the local Depot of Army Printing and Stationery Services.

## 11. *Discipline.*

All Indian Labour is enrolled and will be dealt with under Army Regulations, India, Vol. II, and the Indian Army Act in the usual way.

The Summary Powers (minor punishments) of an O.C. Labour Company are those of a Commanding Officer under Indian Military Law as contained in F.S.R. Part II, Indian Supplement, Chapter XIII, Section 64.

He can also hold a Summary Court Martial and exercise, when sitting as this Court, the large powers given to C.Os. of detachments under the Indian Army Act, *vide* Sec. 63, Chap. XIII, Indian Supplement of F.S.R., Part II.

The powers of an Indian Officer are similar to those specified in Indian Army Regulations, Vol. II.

With regard to corporal punishment, *see* S.S. 630, para. 6 (*g*) and (*h*).

Minor offences committed by Indians should, as a rule, be dealt with by Officers Commanding Companies.

More serious crimes, cases reported by the Police, and charges against white non-commissioned officers will be referred to Officers Commanding Groups, by Officers Commanding Companies.

Proceedings of Courts Martial held on natives should be sent to the D.J.A.G., Indian Troops, G.H.Q., 3rd Echelon, to whom Group Commanders should refer for advice on all questions of Indian Military law. There are special forms for use for Courts Martial, which should always be used—I.A.F. D. 907 " Proceedings of a Summary Court Martial," and I.A.F. F. 956 " Proceedings of a Summary General Court Martial."

Under the Indian Army Act the conditions under which a person is enrolled cannot be altered except with the consent of the person concerned. This applies to Headmen, Assistant Headmen, Interpreters, Clerks, and Mates, and therefore if, for example, a man *has been enrolled* as a Headman he cannot be reduced to an appointment carrying a lower rate of pay.

If, however, a man was enrolled as a Mate and subsequently appointed Headman he can be relegated to the rank of Mate by Summary Award, but not to that of Labourer.

A Labourer originally enrolled who after his enrolment is promoted to a higher grade, or to any appointment, nay be summarily reduced to the grade of Labourer, or to any intermediate grade, by the authority who has power to make the promotion or appointment.

If a man is considered unsuitable for the appointment which he holds and cannot be reduced, his case should be referred to higher authority, with a view to repatriation.

### 12. *Passes.*

Subject to any local orders these should be granted in the discretion of the Company Commander.

No passes should, however, be made available after sunset except for men on duty.

No passes to be signed by any person except the O.C. Company or the officer deputed by him to do so. Passes to be stamped with the Company stamp.

### 13. *Medical Arrangements.*

The Lahore Indian General Hospital at Rouen, with a section at Marseilles, receives Indian Personnel. Local Detention Wards, or Stationary Hospitals, will be established where required.

When men are sent to hospital they should be carefully ticketed with a clear indication of Number, Name, Unit, Group, and nearest Railway Station. Their Service Books should be inspected to see that their names and the number of their Companies are clearly shown. All Kits also should be marked with the man's name and number, and the number of his Company and his Group.

### 14. *Precautions against Injury of Labourers by Explosives.*

As many of the Indian and other Asiatic Companies are employed on Salvage work in former battle areas, it is necessary to order the men before commencing work not to touch any shells, bombs, grenades, fuzes, detonators, &c., that they may find. They should be shown examples of the different kinds of things that are dangerous, and should be told that anyone found deliberately handling any such things will be punished. Notices to this effect should be written out in the vernacular of the Company, or in the several dialects spoken by the men ; and these notices should be posted up where every man can see them. Asiatic labourers when employed on Salvage work should not be allowed to handle explosives.

### 15. *Reports of Injuries.*

Reports of injuries received from accidents with explosives should always be reported on A.F. W. 3428.

In any case of death caused by such accidents a Court of Enquiry must be held (*see* K.R. paras. 668-678 and R. of P., page 637).

### 16. *Burials.*

Attention is drawn to the Instructions to Officers in Extracts from G.R.Os., Part I.

No Indians, other than Christians, should be buried in a British Military, or a French Communal Cemetery, except in cases where there is a plot specially set aside for Indian graves. In back areas every effort should be made to bury in existing Indian cemeteries and not to start new ones.

There are a considerable number of Christians in the I.L.C. These will be buried in the same cemeteries and plots as British soldiers, and crosses will be erected on their graves in the usual way.

Under no circumstances should a cross be erected over the graves of Indians other than Christians. Stakes are provided to take their place. Officers of Graves Registration Units are responsible for reporting immediately any departure from this order, giving the name of the person who caused the cross to be erected.

The same return will be rendered in the case of Indian soldiers as in the case of British.

### 17. *Censoring.*

Os.C. Companies are responsible for the proper censoring of all letters written by the personnel of their Companies. If any O.C. Company is unable to have a letter read and translated to him by a reliable N.C.O., Clerk or Interpreter of his own Company, he should apply to O.C. Group, who will, if possible, have it censored in some other Company of the Group.

Letters are stamped with the censor stamp at Group Headquarters on the signature of the O.C. Company or an officer deputed by him. Only those letters which have been censored by Units should bear a censor stamp.

All letters written in native languages should be tied in bundles, which should be labelled "Indian Labour letters." These bundles should be handed in at any Army or Field Post Office, together with the other correspondence of the unit.

The labels on bundles of letters which cannot be censored by units should be marked "Uncensored."

In addition to the matters mentioned in Censorship Orders for Troops in the Field (*see* Extracts G.R.Os. Part I.) Indians are forbidden :—

(i) To send picture postcards, photographs or pictures.

(ii) To send newspapers or printed matter.

*Addressing of letters to India and adjacent countries.*—As there is considerable difficulty in the delivery of letters addressed to Indians, Burmese and other Asiatics, every letter sent that anticipates a reply should contain an envelope addressed to the sender. The following is the correct form of address :—

*e.g.*, No.    Labourer (Name)

56th (Khasi) Company,

Indian Labour Corps,

B.E.F., France.

Nothing else should be added to the address.

Os.C. Companies should keep the Indian Base Post Office, BOULOGNE, informed of all changes in the personnel of their Units, in sufficient detail to enable mails to be re-directed.

Great care must be taken to prevent letters being posted in the French or Belgian civil post.

## 18. *General Remarks.*

Although some of the men in the Corps come from the Hill Country, it must not be assumed that they can withstand the conditions of a Northern European Winter, unless they are properly looked after and cared for.

The fact that they are now receiving better food than they are probably accustomed to in their own homes will, no doubt, have a beneficial effect on their physique and power of withstanding disease.

Their housing, clothing, and feeding are, therefore matters of first importance, and if neglected their efficiency as Labour Units will be seriously impaired.

European supervision is necessary with all Indians if good results are to be obtained.

Indian Labour should be concentrated as much as possible, in order to reduce the numbers of Europeans required for supervision. The latter should seldom be changed, and this, of course, also applies to the allotment of Indian Labour, which should, if possible, be kept on the same work. It is not economical to detail Indians in small parties.

When dealing with Indians it should be remembered that many an Indian meets only a few white men in the course of a lifetime, and that it is on what he sees of *them* that he forms his opinions of the whole race.

The opinion of an individual Indian spreads among other natives. A single act of injustice may bring about widespread discontent.

Care should be taken that nothing is done to wound the pride or insult the religion of an Indian.

It is a great mistake to imagine that civility or good fellowship towards an Indian is likely to lower the white man in his eyes, so long as the action of the white man is such that he does not lower his own dignity.

The Indian races, generally, have a respect for the soldierly qualities, sporting instincts, and sense of justice of the British, and a knowledge that they are being treated with justice and consideration tends to increase that respect. Discipline must, however, be maintained.

Both the bull and the cow are sacred to all Hindus and Sikhs, and the killing of them is against their religious feelings. Beef should never be given to them.

The Mohammedan will not eat pork. Sheep or goats are generally provided for them. They are slaughtered at the Base in accordance with the requirements of the Mohammedan religion, or regimentally if sent up alive.

### 19. *Suitability for various Employments.*

Full information as regards the suitability of the different Companies for various classes of work, &c., what amount of supervision they require, and whether they contain English-speaking natives, tradesmen, &c., are kept at the Headquarters of the Controller of Labour.

Some of the Companies have shown considerable proficiency at work, which it is believed they had never been employed upon before.

In view of the constant developments resulting from the above, it is considered that any notes which could now be embodied herein might, in a short time, become actually misleading. It has, therefore, been decided to omit all information of this nature.

When Companies are moved to new areas, Labour Commandants and Group Commanders will be furnished with all information available.

## CHAPTER XIX.—CHINESE LABOUR.

### 1. The Establishment of a Chinese Labour Company is :—

| | PERSONNEL. | | | | | | | | | |
|---|---|---|---|---|---|---|---|---|---|---|
| | British. | | | | | Chinese. | | | | |
| DETAIL. | Officers. | Warrant Officers. | Clerks. | Staff-Sergts. and Sergts. | Rank and File. | Interpreters. | Rank and File. | Total. | RIDING HORSES. | BICYCLES. |
| Major or Captain ... | 1 | ... | ... | ... | ... | ... | ... | 1 | (*f*) | (*f*) |
| Subalterns ... ... | 4 | ... | ... | ... | ... | ... | ... | 4 | ... | 2 |
| Coy. Sergt.-Major ... | ... | 1 | ... | ... | ... | ... | ... | 1 | ... | ... |
| Coy. Qr.-Mr.-Sergeant .. | .. | .. | ... | 1 | .. | ... | ... | 1 | ... | ... |
| Sergeants... ... ... | .. | ... | ... | 8 | ... | ... | ... | 8 | ... | ... |
| Corporals ... ... | ... | ... | .. | ... | 9 (*a*) | ... | ... | 9 | ... | ... |
| Chinese Interpreter Clerk | ... | ... | ... | ... | ... | 1 | ... | 1 | ... | ... |
| Chinese Coolies ... ... | ... | ... | ... | ... | ... | ... | 470 (*b*) | 470 | ... | ... |
| Chinese Batmen ... | ... | ... | ... | ... | ... | ... | 5 | 5 | ... | ... |
| Total ... ... | 5 | 1 | ... | 9 | 9 | 1 | 475 | 500 | ... | 2 |

A Labour Company (Chinese) consists of a Headquarters and 4 Platoons, each under a Subaltern.

Each Platoon consists of 2 Sections, each under a Sergeant.

(*a*) Includes 1 Corporal Cook.

(*b*) Includes 1 Head Ganger and 31 Gangers Classes I, II and III.

(*f*) 1 riding horse or bicycle for the O.C. Company is allowed in cases where the G.O.C. Formation considers that such an issue is necessary.

Transport.—The same as for a British Labour Company.

### 2. *Depot.*

The Base Depot is at Noyelles-sur-Mer, 9 miles from Abbeville. Postal Address : A.P.O. S. 1.

The Headquarters, C.L.C., are at present also at Noyelles.

All Chinese on arrival in France are taken direct to the Depot, where they remain a minimum of five days for equipment and organisation.

There is an O.C. Depot with the usual Depot Staff.

Officer i/c Chinese Records and Chinese Censors are at Noyelles.

The records of British Personnel of the Chinese Labour Corps are kept by the Labour Corps Section, D.A.G., 3rd Echelon.

### 3. *Extracts from Contract made with the Chinese on engagement in China.*

(*a*) The Chinese must not be employed within the danger zone.

(b) The labourer* is entitled to food, clothing summer and winter, housing and fuel, and medical attendance free.

(c) Duration of employment.—Three years, determinable by the Government at the end of first year on six months' clear notice. The Government can terminate contract on insubordination or misconduct of the labourer and can repatriate him at Government expense.

(d) Stoppage of Wages.—If a labourer goes sick and is unable to work, his daily pay is stopped so long as he is incapacitated from work. He will, however, be accommodated and receive food and medical attention free. If incapacity does not exceed six weeks, the monthly allotment in China will continue to be paid. If his incapacity exceeds six weeks, the monthly allotment will cease beyond the six weeks and will not be continued until work is resumed.

(e) A breach of the Regulations or hindering or delay of work on the part of the labourer involves the forfeiture of daily pay. The loss of pay for 28 days or more will lead to a stoppage of the monthly allotment for the period of work missed or delayed.

(f) Holidays.—At the option of the British authorities. Contract is for seven days' work per week.

### 4. Hours of Work.

No ruling as to hours for other Labour in France cancels the terms of the Chinese contract to work 10 hours per day, which must be remembered if the Chinese make claims for overtime.

If overtime is necessary and performed, a shorter period of work should be arranged for the following day.

Weather only of an exceptional nature should be allowed to interfere with work, and such days must be paid for. When no work is provided labourers must be paid full rates. Rest days are paid for at full rates; there is no half-day rate.

### 5. Chinese Savings Bank.

A Savings Bank for Chinese has now been established (G.R.O. 4574).

### 6. Casualty Returns.

(a) For White Personnel, A.F. B. 213 in duplicate is rendered. One copy should be sent to D.A.G., G.H.Q., 3rd Echelon, together with A.F. B. 2069 (Offence Report), and the other to H.Q., C.L.C., A.P.O. S. 1.

This return is rendered on Sundays.

---

* In the following notes the term "Labourer" includes all the grades of enrolled Chinese, unless otherwise stated.

(b) For *Chinese* Personnel special forms are used, which can be obtained from Officer i/c Chinese Records, to whom they should be sent in duplicate. They are to be rendered on Saturday, made up to, and for, Thursday in each week. They must be numbered consecutively. Any requirements for skilled personnel should be shown on the back of this form, the numbers required for each trade being shown separately.

(c) When the last Thursday in a month is within two days of the last day of the month the Casualty Return should be made up to the end of the month, and be rendered two days late.

For any longer period than two days after the last Thursday, an additional Casualty Return should be rendered up to, and including, the last day of the month.

" Nil " Casualty Returns are required.

(d) In cases of death, separate Casualty Returns for each death will be rendered in duplicate.

(e) An entry should be made on a Casualty Return for every Labourer who is absent *on the last day of the month.*

For those Labourers who are still absent on the 1st of the following month, a new period of absence will begin.

This is the only exception to the rule that Labourers should not appear on the Casualty Return until they return to work.

(f) Any previous error in a nominal roll, or casualty return, can be corrected in a subsequent casualty return by an entry thus :—

> Labourer No. —— shown in Nominal Roll, dated ——, should read Ganger III.
>
> Labourer No. —— shown on Casualty Return No. 11 should read Ganger I, No. ——.

### 7. *Courts of Inquiry.*

A Court of Inquiry will be appointed if considered necessary to investigate cases of injury to Chinese. Attention is directed to paras. Nos. 666 to 678 of K.R. As the proceedings of these Courts will possibly be used as a basis for settlement of claims for compensation, the greatest care must be taken to comply with these regulations. Cases of injury should be reported on A.F. W. 3428, in accordance with instructions on the back of this form (*see* G.R.O. 3355).

### 8. *Admissions to Chinese General Hospital at Noyelles.*

When Chinese are admitted to the Chinese General Hospital at Noyelles, either direct from Companies at work or from any source, they will be taken on the strength of the Depot, C.L.C., from the date of admission to the Chinese General Hospital at Noyelles.

The O.C. Depôt will immediately notify the Company Commander by letter giving the registered numbers and dates of admission, to enable the Company Commander to strike the Labourer off his strength. The O.C. Depôt will mark up the work ticket for the intermediate period. The O.C. Company concerned will then show such Chinese in his Casualty Return, as transferred to Depôt on the date notified.

On their discharge from the Chinese General Hospital at Noyelles, these Chinese will rejoin their original Companies, as far as circumstances permit.

## 9. *Procedure to be adopted when Labourers are Transferred from one Unit to another.*

(a) Except in the case of Nos. 1 to 7 and 10 to 16 Chinese Labour Companies, cross-postings of Chinese who are certificated as skilled may be carried out in these Groups by Officers Commanding Labour Groups with the approval of Labour Commandants in Army Areas and Base and Area Commandants in the L. of C. area. A copy of the order issued by O.C. Labour Group for such cross-postings, showing registered numbers of Chinese reposted, will be rendered to Adviser Chinese Labour under G.R.O. 3861.

(b) When an O.C. Labour Group has any Chinese certificated as skilled surplus to requirements in his Group, he will cause the registered numbers of such to be recorded on the last page of A.F. B. 213 rendered to H.Q. Chinese Labour Corps weekly by each Chinese Company Commander. (*See* G.R.Os. 4314, 4360 and 4395.)

## 10. *Camps.*

(a) Enclosures for the Chinese should not be contiguous to white men's camps; if this is unavoidable galvanised iron should be put up. Otherwise galvanised iron is unnecessary.

(b) When there is more than one Chinese Company in the same camp, they should have separate enclosures, with separate cookhouses, latrines, ablution places, and storehouse or tent.

(c) The necessity for enclosures when the Chinese are employed on purely temporary work, and isolated from towns, will be decided on each occasion by Army Headquarters or by H.Q. L. of C. Area.

## 11. *Accommodation.*

H.Q. C.L.C. will be notified when it is proposed to construct accommodation for Chinese, in order that an officer from the H.Q. C.L.C. may be sent to report to, and to advise, the officer responsible for selecting the site, and providing accommodation.

(a) Huts or tents. If in tents, 14 men per tent. If in huts, 4 ft. wall space per man in huts less than 20 ft. wide or 40 sq. ft.

in huts 20 ft. wide or more; except in emergency when, from lack of other shelter, the accommodation may be reduced to 25 sq. ft. Stoves in winter, of any suitable pattern, but not in summer.

*Beds.* In buildings or huts with wooden floors beds are not required. No paillasses required.

(*b*) Cookhouse. One for each Company. A structure sufficiently large to cook for 500 Chinese. Concrete floors, of course, preferable, but this depends on circumstances and the nature of the soil. Six Soyer stoves and 75 kettles per Company are included in the Mobilization Store Table.

About 6 Chinese large open metal bowls for cooking chuppaties. These are supplied from the Depôt.

Four barrack tables for working up flour on.

If Water-jacketed Rice Boilers are not obtainable, the best way to cook rice is in camp kettles over trenches (*see* illustration).

(*c*) *Bath House* and drying room can be combined.

(*d*) *Ablution Huts.* Accommodation for 12 per cent. of strength.

(*e*) *Water Supply* from taps in the enclosure, supplied from tanks or water mains, when available; otherwise Water Carts will be used.

(*f*) *Latrines*, for 5 per cent. of strength, with buckets.

(*g*) *Storehouse* should be provided for food, clothing, equipment and tools, dimensions in proportion to men.

(*h*) *Offices and Orderly Room* should be provided outside the enclosure.

(*i*) *Canteens.* A Y.M.C.A. hut if possible, with European and Chinese commodities, but no intoxicants.

(*j*) *Guard Room.* A wired enclosure for prisoners outside and, if possible, 40 or 50 yards from the enclosure. One or two bell tents inside the enclosure for prisoners, or tent d'abris constructed of corrugated iron, or any suitable material, and two tents outside for Police—one for British Police and one for Chinese Police.

When two or more Companies are together, separate lock-ups for each Company are not required.

(*k*) *Destructor.* Either inside or outside enclosure.

(*l*) *Lighting* to be by hurricane lamps, in charge of men specially trained.

*British Personnel.* In the interests of discipline, sleeping accommodation, latrines, ablution rooms and cookhouses for Officers and white personnel must be well removed from, and outside, the Chinese enclosures.

The above requirements apply chiefly to semi-permanent enclosures. When enclosures are not provided for the Chinese the same principles will be followed as far as possible.

### 12. *Notes on Cooking Rice.*

The " water-jacketed rice cookers " in use in the Chinese Depot are good for cooking rice, but where these are not available, Army camp kettles should be used with a trench fire, as shown in the sketch below. A kettle is placed in each compartment, and after about 20 minutes the kettle nearest the fire is then moved to the compartment at the far end of the trench and left to steam there, the remaining kettles being moved up one. The next kettle over the fire is moved in about another 20 minutes. One labourer can handle 10 kettles, and no rice is wasted by burning. Soyer stoves and farm boilers are good for tea and hot water, but if used for rice a proportion is wasted by burning.

The following is a design for a trench fire for cooking rice :—

A Trench.

B Support for camp kettles, to raise well away from bottom of trench. Can be made with pieces of corrugated iron, laid crossways, and covered with earth.

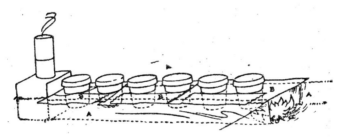

*Note.*—Opening should face prevailing wind. Trench should slope upward from fire to chimney.

### 13. *Military Ranks.*

These should not be used in any correspondence or returns relating to the Chinese. A labourer is either a Head Ganger, a Ganger, Class I, II, or III, or a Coolie.

Interpreters and Dressers are called Interpreters, Class I or II, or Field Interpreters (graded as Gangers II, for pay), and Dressers, Class I, II or III.

### 14. *Stationery.*

Indents for ordinary Army stationery should be sent to Local Depot of Army Printing and Stationery Depots.

The following special stationery can be obtained from O. i/c Records, C.L.C. :—

> Work Tickets.
> Monthly Pay Lists.
> Chinese Envelopes.
> Books of Daily Work Sheets.
> Identification Forms.
> Casualty Returns for Chinese.

Os.C. Companies should be as economical as possible owing to the shortage of paper.

### 15. *Group Commanders.*

All Companies are under their respective Labour Group Commanders, through whom all correspondence should pass.

### 16. *Reinforcements.*

Will be supplied on instructions being received at the Depot from the A.G.

### 17. *Clothing.*

*See* G.R.Os. 2799 (as amended by G.R.O. 3489), 2895 and 3001.

All Chinese Companies, before leaving the Depot at Noyelles, are equipped—either in China, or locally—with all articles of equipment and clothing necessary for many months to come.

Loss of clothing is mainly a disciplinary matter, and can generally be stopped by heavy forfeitures of pay.

Articles of clothing and equipment alleged to be " lost " can be replaced on repayment in the usual way, by using A.F. W. 3069, but a forfeiture of pay should often be inflicted in addition. The replacement of articles on repayment on A.F. W. 3069 necessitates corresponding entries on Casualty Returns.

Chinese do not lose their clothes, but the good prices obtainable from civilians induce them to do so.

The Chinaman is by nature careful of his clothing, and indiscriminate issues will make him careless and wasteful.

Free issues should be made to units and not to individuals.

Tools for tailors and shoemakers are provided in the Mobilization Store Table, and tailors' and shoemakers' shops should be installed in each Company.

### 18. *Rations, Forage, Fuel and Light.*

*See* G.R.O. 2523 and S.S. 571, as amended by current G.R.Os.

European personnel receive rations as for British troops.

Interpreters may select either the Chinese scale or the scale authorized from time to time for British troops. Once having made their choice, however, they must adhere to it.

### 19. *Mobilization Store Table.*

A.F. G. 1098/388, dated January, 1918.

### 20. *Discipline.*

(*a*) Generally speaking, the Chinese give little trouble ; theft is the most common offence, drunkenness is rare. Chinese found wandering about, or any arrested, will be sent to the nearest Chinese Camp.

(*b*) A system of identification by finger prints has been adopted and each Company Commander has the necessary apparatus.

(*c*) All British ranks are strictly forbidden to supply any intoxicating liquors to Labourers.

All Estaminets and Cafés are out of bounds for Chinese. *See* G.R.O. 2745.

(*d*) When more than one Chinese Company are encamped together, Company Commanders should arrange amongst themselves for a similar scale of punishments for similar offences committed by the men in their respective companies.

The Group Commander can assist in this matter, without unduly interfering with the Company Commander's position. The awards of Company Commanders should be final, any mitigation of sentence by the Group Commander (unless an evident illegality has been committed), should be avoided. If unavoidable the mitigation, or remission, should be given effect to as emanating from the Company Commander.

Company Commanders should remember the limitations of their power, reserving the maximum penalty for the most serious offence which they can deal with.

(*e*) About 3 White N.C.Os. should be detailed as Police, assisted by a certain number of Chinese Police. These latter by themselves are unsatisfactory unless supported, and are a frequent cause of trouble by their natural desire to enrich themselves at the expense of the Labourers.

The following is extracted from Instructions issued by the A.G. in his B/6312/4 of 27/6/17 :—

(*a*) All Chinese are subject to military law under Sec. 176 (9) Army Act.

On arrival at NOYELLES, the principles of discipline under military law and the method of lodging complaints are explained to each contingent. Verbal complaints may be made in the usual way, and in special cases written petitions may be addressed to the Head of the Chinese.

(*b*) Applications for Courts Martial will be submitted by Os.C. Companies to O.C. Labour Group.

(*c*) If it is decided to assemble a Court Martial, the convening officer will inform the Adviser, C.L.C., who will submit the name of an officer to act as President and will detail an Interpreter. The convening officer will appoint two other members of the Court, one of whom will be an officer of the C.L.C.

(*d*) Members of a Court Martial should be familar with Chinese habits and customs, *e.g.* :—

- (i) Chinamen are very loth to give evidence, as by so doing enmity is incurred.
- (ii) Chinese witnesses should be " declared " according to native custom. They can be sworn, but an " oath " has slight moral weight with the Chinese.
- (iii) Interpreters at a Court Martial should always be officers of the C.L.C.

(*e*) When any offence has been committed in respect of which forfeiture of pay as provided above would not be sufficient, but which would normally in the case of soldiers be dealt with by C.O., and would be adequately met by a sentence of not more than 28 days' Field Punishment No. 1, the offender can be tried by F.G.C.M., conducted in the following manner, if the O.C. Company is of opinion that owing to the exigencies of the service it is not practicable to deal with the case otherwise (S.S. 630a) :—

- (i) The Court will be convened by O.C. Company.
- (ii) O.C. Company will sit as President.
- (iii) He need only appoint one other officer to sit with him (*see* Rules of Procedure 107*a*).
- (iv) No summary of evidence taken before trial.
- (v) The charge will be briefly stated (*see* examples on page 702, Manual of Military Law).
- (vi) Only shortest possible record of evidence to be taken at the trial.
- (vii) A.F. A. 3 will invariably be used and the following certificate will be written on page 1 of this Army Form, namely, after the words " 3. Three officers, having more than one year's service," the words " 4. An officer other than myself as President," and after the words " For the following reasons, namely," the words " the want of qualified officers and great urgency."
- (viii) The proceedings will be forwarded to the confirming officer, who will normally be the Labour Group Commander.
- ix) The proceedings after they have been confirmed and promulgated will at once be forwarded through the usual channels to headquarters of the Army or Lines of Communication Area.

(x) More important cases, where the offence, if proved, would require punishment in excess of 28 days' Field Punishment No. 1, will be dealt with by F.G.C.M., convened and confirmed in the ordinary way (*see* S.S. 630, para. 9).

(*f*) The following punishments cannot be awarded to a Chinese Labourer by Court Martial, and if passed will be inoperative :—

(i) Fines, except for drunkenness.

(ii) C.B. or Forfeiture of Pass. A pass can obviously be withdrawn by the C.O.

(iii) Reduction from Ganger to Coolie. Such reduction can be effected by the O.C. Company, independently of trial (*see* S.S. 630*b*).

(*g*) Procedure on Courts Martial :—

(i) The accused should be described as Coolie (or Ganger) No....... .........Company, Chinese Labour Corps.

(ii) A plea and finding must be entered in respect of each charge on which an accused person is tried.

(iii) When an accused pleads not guilty, the evidence of witnesses must be taken orally ; in the case of white witnesses on oath, and in the case of coloured witnesses, in whatever way is most binding on their conscience. So-called " documentary " evidence of Medical Officers, Military Police, or other absent witnesses is inadmissible for the prosecution.

(iv) A short record of the defence should be made.

(v) A Convening Officer cannot appoint any officer senior to himself as President or Member of a Court Martial.

(vi) If the O.C. Labour Group happens for the time being to be below the rank of Field Officer, he cannot confirm the proceedings (R.P. 120 (*e*) (ii).

(*h*) Interpreters and Dressers are under the Army Act in the same way as Labourers, but must not be treated as Labourers, as they are as a rule drawn from a superior class. For continual misdemeanours they may be returned to the Depot at NOYELLES for " Further instruction " in their duties, or possibly for repatriation to China under the power vested in the Adviser C.L.C. They should not be degraded or promoted without reference to the Adviser, C.L.C. In most cases they are respectable Chinese citizens, and should never be addressed as Labourers.

### 21. *Passes.*

#### *See* G.R.O. 3101.

It must be remembered that the Chinese are serving on a long contract, and that it is desirable to grant them passes, so long as it does not interfere with their work. If sanction is given through the Labour Group Commander for the issue of passes, they will be granted at the discretion of Company Commanders upon the following principles, subject to any modifications imposed by special local conditions :—

(i) Not more than 10 per cent. of the strength of a Company to be given passes on one day. They should be under the charge of a Ganger in parties of not less than 12. In Army Areas they must be in groups of not less than five Coolies, each group to be under the charge of a white N.C.O. (A.C./7/10 (P.S.), 3.4.18).

(ii) No man classified by the Medical authorities as " Trachoma Z " to be allowed out on pass. A dry canteen in each " Trachoma Z " Camp should be provided.

(iii) The limit of distance from Camp must vary with local circumstances. The essential point is that Chinese have access to local shops. A 3-mile limit should never be exceeded, except for some specific cause or duty.

(iv) No passes for Chinese to be made available for later than half-an-hour after sunset.

(v) No passes to be signed by any person except the O.C. Company, or the Officer deputed by him to do so. Passes to be stamped with the Company stamp.

(vi) The Company control to be such as to ensure that passes are taken from Chinese immediately on their return to their Camp and destroyed.

It is generally possible to fix " Camp Precincts " within which passes are not required. By this is meant the immediate vicinity (300 or 400 yards) of the Camp. The limits should be clearly explained to the Chinese, and, if they " break bounds," the privilege should be withdrawn. No villages are to be included in Camp precincts.

## 22. *Canteens.*

A Shop or Canteen is a necessity.

Application for Canteens will be submitted in the usual way to Labour Group H.Q., and by them to H.Q. of Formations. The O.C. Company concerned should provide accommodation either in existing buildings, or tents, as the erection of huts takes considerable time. The management should be left in the hands of the Officials of the Y.M.C.A.

## 23. *Medical Arrangements.*

The Chinese Base Hospital is at NOYELLES.

If Os.C. Companies require information as to Hospital arrangements reference should be made to the Group Commander.

When casualties or accidents occur, one or two friends should always be allowed to accompany the man to the Hospital; this is specially important in the case of a serious accident, as if the man dies on the way suspicion is aroused.

Chinese have strong objections to post-mortem examinations.

Trachoma is prevalent among the Chinese. Steps are taken to segregate these cases as far as possible by the formation of special Trachoma Companies to receive them.

All cases of trachoma will be reported at once by Labour Group Headquarters to Headquarters, Chinese Labour Corps, direct, a copy of the report being submitted to Labour Commandants in the case of Army Areas, and to Base or Area Commandants in the case of the L. of C. Area.

These cases will be removed to No. 3 Native Labour General Hospital or transferred to a "Z" (Trachoma) Company, under instructions to be issued by H.Q., Chinese Labour Corps. Cases of conjunctivitis will be treated locally and remain with their Companies (vide G.R.O. 4497).

### 24. Identification.

The finger prints of all Chinese who die through any cause, are to be taken and forwarded to Officer i/c Chinese Records (A.P.O. S. 1, B.E.F.).

### 25. Burials.

When new land is required for burial grounds, the Director of Graves Registration and Inquiries, G.H.Q., should be given the longest possible notice in order that he may make the necessary arrangements under G.R.O 1437. Should a site be selected by any other procedure liability for rent may be incurred, and it may be necessary ultimately to exhume the bodies.

The ideal site to secure repose and drive away evil spirits is on sloping ground with a stream below, or gully down which water always or occasionally passes.

The grave should not be parallel to the N., S., E. or W. This is specially important to Chinese Mohammedans. It should be about 4 feet deep, with the head towards the hill and the feet towards the water. A mound of earth about 2 feet high is piled over the grave.

The graves will be registered under the orders of the Director of Graves Registration and Inquiries, but the Chinese should also be allowed to mark them by erecting a wooden tablet at the foot of the grave, stating the name, age, province and village in China of the deceased. The O.C. Labour Group will render to the D.A.D. Graves Registration and Inquiries of the Army, or L. of C. Area, concerned a burial return showing the registered number and date of death of every Chinaman dying in his Group. The Graves Registration Unit concerned will then erect a stake bearing the registered number of the Labourer and the date of death.

Chinese quite realise that ideal grave sites are not always obtainable in foreign countries and raise no objection. Chinese should not be buried in Christian cemeteries unless it is impracticable to provide special cemeteries for them, in which case they may be buried in a corner of a military or a communal cemetery in such a way that their graves are not completely surrounded by graves of Europeans. Under ordinary circumstances special cemeteries cannot be provided except in places where there is good reason to anticipate at least 50 burials.

Whenever possible, the friends of the deceased should be allowed access to, and to handle, the corpse, as they like to dress it and show marks of respect.

### 26. *Censoring of Correspondence.*

All letters written by the Chinese are to be sent to the Chinese Labour Base Depot for censoring. They should be placed in sealed bags and directed to Chinese Censor, A.P.O. S. 1.

Great care must be taken to prevent letters being posted in the French or Belgian civil post.

Application to the Censor to translate Chinese writings is forbidden.

In addition to the matters forbidden in the Postal Censorship Regulations, the Chinese are forbidden to send by post :—

    (i) Picture postcards, photographs, or pictures.

    (ii) Newspapers or printed matter.

### 27. *Notes on Supervision of Work by Officers and N.C.Os.*

Constant supervision on the part of Officers and N.C.Os. is essential to the performance of good work, but the supervision should approximate as closely as possible to labour conditions in China.

Whenever possible Chinese should be employed by themselves, and not where they are in a position to judge or criticise the same class of work performed by white men (*see* G.R.O. 2828).

The Chinese Ganger is the most important link between the Officers and the Labourers, and his position should be clearly defined and upheld.

The responsibility and use of the Chinese Ganger should begin from the day of arival at the Depot, and his " face " should be carefully considered. Nagging at or abusing Gangers before Labourers always leads to bad work and distrust. If a Ganger is inefficient he should be degraded.

The best work is always accomplished by giving definite tasks to the Chinese Ganger, and making him directly responsible for the carrying out of the work. Details as to the moment to prise up, lift, shoulder and move off with baulks, rails, &c., should be left to the Chinese Ganger. The same applies with regard to the simultaneous lowering of heavy loads carried by gangs. A heavy bodily strain is imposed during these operations, which are not expedited, but rather retarded, when every movement is directed by the Europeans in charge. Possible subsequent strain and injury to the workers may be laid by them to the charge of the white man ordering details of movement.

The white N.C.O. should, generally speaking confine himself to reporting individual shirkers and unsatisfactory gangs and Gangers. He should closely observe the gangs when at work, and check irregularities and obvious misconduct or idleness. He must render frequent verbal reports on the work of the Gangers and Labourers to the officers in charge of working parties, in order that unsatisfactory gangs may be frequently visited, and dealt with by officers who understand the Chinese.

Unless the work is of a continuous nature, Officers Commanding Companies should ascertain, as far in advance as possible, the place and description of new work. The new working ground should be visited by an Officer of the Company, accompanied by an N.C.O. and 1 or more Gangers, prior to setting the gangs to work. Details of work could then be settled with the Gangers and Guides, who can be at their stations before the working parties arrive. This method should result in an economy of time and labour.

A Chinese Company, on arrival from the Depot, should work together during the first fortnight, as far as possible, and should not be split up into small parties.

## 28. *General Remarks.*

It is essential that discipline should be maintained by the Officers and N.C.Os. of the C.L.C., and the Chinese should be made to understand this from the commencement.

For the guidance of Officers and N.C.Os. the following facts regarding the Chinese should be noted :—

(a) He comes here primarily for money.

(b) He is a rigid adherent to his contract though agreeable to modifications, *e.g.*, task work, if advantageous to him.

(c) He is unequalled as a judge of human character; the best procurable class of white overseer is therefore necessary to obtain the best results.

(d) He is fond of litigation and lodging complaints, and, though he can be " sworn," his evidence must be accepted with considerable reserve.

(e) He is not addicted to crimes of violence or drunkenness, but is an inveterate gambler.

(f) Undue familiarity between any white personnel and Chinese employees is to be deprecated as subversive of discipline.

No Chinese speaking persons, other than those belonging to the Chinese Labour Companies, should be allowed in canteens or recreation huts, and the entry of all strangers to the camp should be strictly forbidden.

The Chinese, in China, are accustomed to seek redress of grievances by means of written petitions ; locked petition boxes should be provided. Precautions should be taken to see that this is not abused or used frivolously.

Chinese are accustomed to " Proclamations." These, when approved by A.G., should be posted on a notice board in Chinese Compounds. They will be prepared at H.Q., C.L.C., and issued to Group Commanders.

There is a staff of Chinese speaking " technical officers " at H.Q., C.L.C., who may be attached to companies temporarily, under the orders of the Adviser, C.L.C.

## CHAPTER XX.—OTHER COLOURED LABOUR COMPANIES.

1. The Egyptian Labour Corps has been withdrawn and the South African Native Labour Corps is being withdrawn from France. It is not thought necessary therefore to give in this book information as to their Establishments, &c. Those facts were originally published as separate appendices to " Notes for Officers of Labour Companies of the Cape Coloured Battalion. There is only one South African Labour Unit in France ; it is composed of " Cape Boys." The personnel have been enlisted. The unit has acquired special proficiency in handling ammunition.

2. *Fijian Labour Contingent.*

No Establishment has been laid down. The contingent now in France consists of :—

> 2 Officers, European.
> 5 N.C.Os., European.
> 1 N.C.O., Native.
> 100 O.R., Natives.

*Terms of Service.*—All ranks were engaged in Fiji at the same rate of pay as for British Infantry from date of enrolment till date of discharge upon return to Fiji.

*Accounting.*—As for British Units.

*Casualty Returns.*—As for British Units.

*Accommodation.*—Same as for British Units, but huts with stoves in winter are essential.

*Scale of Clothing.*—*See* G.R.Os. 2799 and 4477.

*Canteens.*—May use " dry side " of British Canteens.

*Mobilization Store Table,* A.F. G. 1098/388, dated January, 1918.

*Discipline.*—Under the Army Act as enlisted soldiers.

*Medical Arrangements.*—Same as for British Troops.

*Burials.*—They are Christians.

*Censoring.*—Can be done by Company Officers.

*General Remarks.*—The contingent contains a few winchmen. All are good boatmen and good wharf labourers, with a proportion of stevedores. There are a few good clerks among them. They are educated and intelligent. They are well behaved and well disciplined.

## APPENDIX " A."

When a Company moves from one Group to another the O.C. Company, will on arrival, send in a return in the Form shown below. The object of this return is to enable the Group Commander to render the Company assistance if required

### RETURN TO BE RENDERED TO GROUP H.Q. BY Os.C. COMPANIES ON MOVING INTO A NEW GROUP.

No............. LABOUR COMPANY.

Rationed up to and including...............................................1918.

*Location.* (Give map reference if necessary.)

MARCHING IN STATE.

|  | Officers. | W.Os. and N.C.Os. | O.Rs. | Remarks accounting for men on Command. |
|---|---|---|---|---|
| Company Strength ... |  |  |  |  |
| Attached    ...    ... |  |  |  |  |
| Total ...    ...    ... <br> On Leave  ...    ... |  |  |  |  |
| On Command    ... |  |  |  |  |
| In Hospital    ... |  |  |  |  |
| Grand Total ...    ... |  |  |  |  |

*Note.*—In the case of P. of W. Cos. the Escort and P. of W. must be shown separately.

---

## OFFICERS.

| Rank. | Name and Initials. | With Co. On Leave, Hospital, &c. | Date of Commission. | Leave. Date last left England. | Medical Classification and Date. | Age. | Civil Occupation. | REMARKS. State technical subjects in which Officers are qualified. |
|---|---|---|---|---|---|---|---|---|
|  |  |  |  |  |  |  |  |  |

## TRANSPORT AND EQUIPMENT.

| G.S. Wagons. | Water Carts. | Hand Carts. | Bicycles. | Horses. | | | Mules. | Remarks accounting for any other vehicle in possession. | Tents. |
|---|---|---|---|---|---|---|---|---|---|
|  |  |  |  | Riding. | H.D. | L.D. |  |  |  |
|  |  |  |  |  |  |  |  |  |  |

Are any indents outstanding?  If so, give short particulars, showing, in bulk, articles required.

Leave statement as on.............................................1918.

O.R. entitled to leave and without leave for over

| 18 Mos. | 17 Mos. | 16 Mos. | 15 Mos. | 14 Mos. | 13 Mos. | 12 Mos. | 11 Mos. | 10 Mos. | 9 Mos. |
|---|---|---|---|---|---|---|---|---|---|
| (a) | (b) | (c) | (d) | (e) | (f) | (g) | (h) | (i) | (j) |
|  |  |  |  |  |  |  |  |  |  |

(a) should be included in (b), (b) should be included in (c), (c) should be included in (d), and so on.

ND - #0522 - 270225 - C0 - 180/125/7 - PB - 9781908487674 - Matt Lamination